Woodworking Business

How to Make Six Figures Selling Your Wood Crafts and Projects

Alyssa and Garrett Garner

Copyright © 2024 by Alyssa and Garrett Garner

All rights reserved.

No part of this book may be reproduced in any form or by any electronic or mechanical means, including information storage and retrieval systems, without written permission from the author, except for the use of brief quotations in a book review.

Disclaimer

Note from the authors: *Below is the standard disclaimer that books like this typically include. To summarize in our own words, we would like you to know that starting or running a business of any kind comes with inherent risk. If you choose to take the leap, you alone are responsible for the actions and choices you make in your business. While we wish you all the success in the world, we can't make any guarantees that the steps outlined here will have any particular outcome for you, as results are based on many factors. Always consider your decisions carefully, while also maintaining a healthy dose of optimism!*

The information in this book is for informational and educational purposes only. It should not be construed as business, tax, or legal advice of any kind. All information and resources found in this book are based on the opinions of the authors alone unless otherwise noted.

The authors of this book assume no responsibility or liability for any consequence resulting directly or indirectly from any action or inaction you take based on the information found in this book.

While the authors have made every effort to provide accurate information at the time of publication, they do not assume any responsibility for errors or changes that occur after publication.

This book is intended to be used only as a general guide, and not as a sole source of information on the subject matter. Always consult a licensed professional before attempting any techniques outlined in this book.

Congrats!

Congratulations on picking up this book! You currently hold in your hands the keys to successfully launching a profitable woodworking business.

We're SO excited to hear what you think! Once you've finished the book, we would love it if you'd leave an honest review on Amazon.

Your review provides valuable feedback and helps us bring more books and resources to you. We appreciate your support!

Contents

Introduction	ix
1. Woodworking 101	1
2. Wood Crafts to Sell	9
3. Branding	17
4. Photography	23
5. Packaging and Shipping	31
6. Pricing	39
7. Selling In Person at Craft Shows, Events, and More	47
8. Selling Online through Etsy, Amazon, and More	59
9. Six-Figure Marketing	73
10. Business Fundamentals (LLC, Permits, Taxes, and More)	89
11. Scaling to Six Figures	99
12. High-End Selling (Galleries, Interior Designers, and More)	109
You Can Do It!	115
Other Titles by Alyssa and Garrett Garner	117
Resources	119
About the Authors	121

Introduction

If you've dreamed of turning your love of woodworking into a profitable business, you've come to the right place!

In this book, you'll learn how to make a six-figure income selling your wood crafts and projects to customers who are excited to buy from you. You'll learn how to create a profitable product line, expand your market reach, sell on multiple platforms, and so much more.

Whether you're just starting out or you've sold a few pieces before and are looking to scale, this book will help you turn your passion into profit faster than you could ever imagine!

There's a ton of opportunity in the woodworking industry and the income potential is truly staggering. In fact, wood product manufacturing is projected to reach $9.7 billion by the end of 2024. The top 50 companies only command about 30 percent of the market, leaving ample opportunity for small and new businesses.

There are many unique advantages to starting a woodworking business, including:

- **Flexibility**: You can work on your own schedule and take on the projects that interest you the most. You can even work in your home workshop, garage, or backyard shed.

- **Creativity**: You can express your passion and creativity as an artisan. You can be your own boss and turn your hobby into a successful career. Using your hands to create products that are appreciated and loved by others is a source of personal satisfaction and fulfillment.

- **Low Start-Up Costs:** While all businesses require some capital, the woodworking business has low start-up costs compared to most other business ventures. You don't need to rent a large retail space or hire employees. You can get started with just your equipment and materials.

- **Diverse Income Streams:** By selling your products in a variety of ways, you can create several income streams resulting in reliable earnings from your business. For example, you can sell your wood crafts at art shows, online, and to local galleries, ensuring that you'll always have money coming in.

- **High Profit Potential**: With so many opportunities for selling your wood crafts, the potential to make six figures or more with your business is substantial. You just need the right strategies and know-how (hint: you're already ahead of the game just by picking up this book!).

In sum, woodworking is a great opportunity for those who wish to follow their passion, while maintaining a flexible schedule and high earnings.

That being said, all businesses come with hard work and a certain degree of risk. The woodworking industry comes with fluctuating demand, high competition, and the need for adaptability.

With the strategies in this book, you'll learn to mitigate many of the risks and give yourself the best chance of success. If you truly love woodworking and are willing to put in the work, we'll provide the road map to achieving the six-figure business of your dreams!

Ready to get started?

Chapter 1

Woodworking 101

First things first: in order to be successful in the woodworking industry, you'll need to practice and develop your skills.

The woodworkers with the highest earnings are very often those who spent the most time perfecting their craft. They create attractive and high-quality pieces that are in demand and sell at high profit margins.

While this book is primarily about the business side of your woodworking venture, this chapter will provide some basics and tips for improving your craft, so you can create beautiful products that your customers will love!

If you're already an expert at woodworking, feel free to skim this chapter or skip straight to chapter 2.

Workshop

If you're going to build a business around wood crafts, you'll need a consistent and reliable workshop for creating your amazing products!

Your workshop should be a large, well-lit, and dry environment with a safe electrical connection, if using power tools. A garage or backyard shed is a great place to start and will save you significant overhead costs. Consider soundproofing your workspace, so you won't disturb your family or neighbors.

Alternatively, you can look for a community woodshop in your area. These are typically shared woodworking spaces, where you pay a membership fee in exchange for a place to work and access to professional woodworking tools.

You can also consider leasing a private workshop space, but this will drastically increase your overhead costs.

Equipment

The typical initial equipment cost when starting a woodworking business is around $1,500. However, if you're already a passionate woodworker, you may have most or even all of the necessary equipment already.

Below are some of the recommended tools for your woodworking business. These are just basic guidelines as the exact equipment needed will depend on your specific craft.

- Table saw
- Hand saw
- Router
- Drill
- Jointer
- Planer
- Sanders
- Chisels
- Clamps
- Hammer

- Tape measure
- Workbench

While woodworking, even as a hobby, comes with substantial equipment costs, when you're running a business, your woodworking tools will often become tax-deductible resulting in significant savings.

Materials

In addition to equipment and tools, you'll need materials to start your woodworking business.

The basic materials for wood crafts include:

- Wood
- Screws
- Nails
- Dowels
- Glue
- Stain or paint
- Sealants
- Accessories

The initial cost of wood and other materials for your business will vary greatly depending on your craft. Similar to the woodworking equipment discussed above, materials associated with your business are usually tax-deductible. We'll discuss taxes in more detail in chapter 10.

Safety

One of the risks associated with the woodworking industry is possibility of injury. Woodworking is a physically demanding job that often involves sharp tools and heavy machinery. Taking the proper steps to mitigate these risks will ensure that your business is sustainable and set you up for long-term success.

Here are some basic tips to ensure your safety when creating wood crafts or projects:

- Wear safety equipment, including work gloves, safety goggles, earplugs, and steel-toed boots.
- Disconnect power tools when you're not using them. Switch to a single extension cord to reduce hazards.
- Don't wear loose or baggy clothing in the workshop that could get caught on blades or power tools.
- Never use blunt blades or bits. Not only are dull cutting tools dangerous, but they also result in less precise cuts and lower-quality final products.

Education

Just like with any career, when you choose woodworking as your business, it's important to invest in continued education. Even highly skilled woodworkers continue to learn and improve their craft.

With more skill and education, you can often charge higher prices for your work and increase your profit margins. You can mention any certifications or courses you've completed in your marketing materials to demonstrate your professionalism and stand out from the competition.

Below are some reputable sources for education or certification in woodworking. There are paid and free classes available both online and in person, as well as membership opportunities. Most are based in the US unless otherwise noted.

- Architectural Woodwork Institute (US)
- Woodwork Career Alliance of North America (US)
- Association of Woodworking & Furnishing Suppliers (US)
- Woodworkers Guild of America (US)

- British Woodworking Federation (UK)
- Studio Woodworkers Australia (AUS)
- Architectural Woodwork Manufacturers Association of Canada (CA)

You can also explore local workshops and classes in your area. This can be a great way to not only expand your skill set, but also connect with other skilled woodworkers and artisans near you. By engaging with the woodworking community, you can learn new skills, borrow equipment, or even refer business to one another.

Business Considerations

When getting started in the woodworking business, there are some important considerations you'll want to keep in mind:

- Make sure the products you're planning to sell fit comfortably into your vehicle, so you can transport them with ease. This will reduce your overhead costs (i.e., you won't need to rent a separate vehicle in order to start selling) and eliminate barriers to getting started.

- Only sell products that utilize woodworking skills that you've already mastered. You should only sell your best pieces to start. You can always expand your offerings and product line later on, as your skill set grows.

- When you're selling your wood crafts, you want to maintain uniformity and quality throughout your pieces. Keeping a production logbook will make it easy to recreate your products later on, as well as identify any changes or improvements that can be made. For each new product you create, include a photo or sketch alongside notes about materials or tools used, production time, measurements, finished dimensions, and any other relevant information.

- Don't tie up too much of your start-up capital in materials. Start with only what you need for your first batch of inventory. This will generally be five to ten pieces of each product you're planning to sell (unless you make larger, custom pieces). You can always increase materials later on, once you start making sales.

Other Tips

When woodworking becomes your business, the bar for quality is raised compared to when it was a hobby. If you're planning to sell your woodwork and build a six-figure business, every piece needs to be high-quality, precise, and beautiful.

Here are some final tips for creating quality pieces and ensuring your business is a success from the start:

- Always double-check your measurements before cutting a piece of wood. This will help you avoid costly mistakes and wasted materials that could increase your start-up costs.

- Always check your wood for imperfections before

starting any project. This will save you valuable time and resources later on.

- Don't cut all your pieces at once. Measure and cut as you go to avoid any errors.

- When working with wood, you must know the correct moisture content for each piece. If your wood is too dry, it will swell or crack, but if it's too moist, your product can shrink or warp. The Wood H2O app can help you calculate the equilibrium moisture content (EMC) of your wood and help troubleshoot any issues.

Chapter 2

Wood Crafts to Sell

Now that you've graduated woodworking 101, it's time to develop your product line! In this chapter, we'll teach you how to start turning your passion into profit by choosing wood crafts that you enjoy making that also have high sales appeal.

Choosing the right wood crafts to sell is very often the difference between a business that makes six figures and one that barely scrapes by. In order to earn significant income with this venture, you must create products that are in demand and specifically targeted toward an ideal customer base.

Niche

Whether you're a woodworker, a chandler, or a quilter, all six-figure crafters and artisans have one thing in common: they create a profitable product line based on an in-demand niche.

A niche is simply the market segment that's most interested in purchasing your specific products. This is often narrowed down to a subniche that encompasses a smaller, but more targeted, segment of the market.

The more specific your woodworking niche is, the easier it will be to sell your products. The key here is to find a segment of the market that's large enough to have a substantial customer base, but small enough that you can still stand out. The most profitable niches have a demand that's higher than the competition.

When choosing your woodworking niche, consider:

- **Types of projects:** kitchenware, wall art, toys, jewelry, furniture, musical instruments
- **Themes:** religious, wedding, outdoor, nature
- **Styles:** rustic, custom or personalized, high-end, practical, abstract
- **Customer type:** gallery owner, eco-friendly shopper, bargain hunter, interior designer

To choose a niche, you'll first need to think about your own personal strengths and interests within the woodworking trade. Do you like to make small trinkets or larger wall art? Are you skilled at making practical items like bowls and cutting boards or do you prefer making artistic sculptures? Be honest with yourself about where your skill set lies and choose a niche in which you can consistently create quality products.

Next, think about the type of customer that would be in the market for products like yours. Are you looking to appeal to the luxury home owner or is your ideal customer a browser at a craft fair? What is that customer's willingness and ability to pay for your products?

It can be helpful to conceptualize your ideal customer as a real person and nail down the details of their persona. Here are some questions to ask yourself:

- Who is your ideal customer? Take note of some basics like gender, marital status, kids, and income. This can obviously be fluid, but will help solidify the image of your ideal customer in your mind.

- Where does your ideal customer shop? What are some of their favorite shops?

- What social media channels does your ideal customer spend the most time on?

- What blogs or websites does your ideal customer visit?

- What does your ideal customer like to do in their free time?

- What does your ideal customer spend money on (besides the essentials like food and housing)? How much are they willing to spend on these nonessentials?

Finally, make a list of products that would appeal to your ideal customer. For example, if your ideal customer base is conscious homeowners looking to beautify their space, you may sell wooden sculptures, wall art, or even furniture, made from sustainable materials.

Market Research

Once you've brainstormed your niche and ideal customer, the next step is to perform market research to see which products within your niche have the highest demand. The ideal product line for your six-figure woodworking business is one where passion meets profit.

Although you may enjoy creating a specific wood craft, if there isn't adequate demand for your products, then it will be difficult to turn a profit. Business-savvy woodcrafters understand that you must tailor your interests to the current market.

This is where market research comes in. To start, look at which handcrafted products are selling well on popular e-commerce sites, such as Etsy, Amazon Handmade, or eBay.

Here's how to do this research for each e-commerce site:

Etsy

> **1.** Start by browsing the categories on the Etsy home page and choosing one to two that align best with your niche and ideal customer.
>
> **2.** When you click on a category, Etsy will bring up a number of subcategories. For example, if you choose the category "Art & Collectibles", you will find subcategories, such as "Sculpture" or "Dolls & Miniatures".
>
> **3.** When you click on your chosen subcategory, you'll see examples of products that are already popular. Do you see any wood crafts on the first page of search results? If so, how many reviews are there for each product? The placement of the product in search results (not including anything that says "ad"), as well as the number of reviews can be a good indication of whether or not something is selling on Etsy.
>
> For example, in the subcategory "Sculpture", we can immediately see that most of the products on the first page are made from

wood. If you're interested in selling wooden sculptures, this demonstrates very promising demand. A lot of the sculptures on the first page are of birds, such as owls, cardinals, or ravens.

When clicking on the listing for a wooden painted bird sculpture, we can see that it has a bestseller badge (indicating a high sales volume over the past six months), has over 750 reviews for the product, and is currently in 20+ carts.

This indicates a high demand for this type of product (painted bird sculptures) and for wooden sculptures, in general, making this a strong niche on Etsy.

You can perform additional research by typing your product ideas directly into Etsy and seeing what suggestions or results come up.

4. Take note of the competition within your chosen niche. Is it already saturated with too much of the same product? Are all the sellers in the niche doing well or are some clearly lagging behind? How will your product stand out from the ones already available, while still fitting within the expectations for your niche?

In addition to the steps above, you can also use keyword research tools, such as Marmalead or eRank, to find the Etsy search volume of products in your niche. This will give you an idea of which products are most popular by showing how often they're searched by customers. You can compare this to the number of competitors in your niche to understand the overall demand versus the level of competition.

Amazon Handmade

1. Start by going to amazon.com/handmade and browsing through the categories. Alternatively, you can type your niche or product idea into the "Handmade" tab of the Amazon search bar.

2. Click on a product that's in your niche and scroll down to "Product Details". Here, you'll be able to see the Best Sellers Rank (BSR) of the item, as well as the number of reviews.

The Best Sellers Rank indicates the popularity of the item on Amazon. A lower BSR means more sales. Look for niches that have at least three products on the first page of search results with a BSR of #30,000 or less in Handmade Products. This indicates a profitable level of demand for the product.

To perform this research quickly, you can download the free plugin DS Amazon Quick View, an extension that will show the BSR of every product on Amazon right in the search results. This will allow you to see, at a glance, what's selling in Handmade and what isn't.

eBay

1. Type your chosen product into the search bar. Make sure you check the box in the sidebar for "Handmade". Browse the listings that come up.

2. Filter your search results to show only "Sold Items" and "Completed Items". Pay attention to the dates on which the items were sold, so you can determine how often sales are made for this type of product. Compare the number of sold items to the ones that are still listed for sale to ascertain popularity.

Note that while handmade items can be sold on eBay, the highest demand will typically be on Etsy and Amazon Handmade.

Additional Research

In addition to the e-commerce sites above, here are some other ways to determine what's popular and selling in the woodworking industry:

- Expand your search to Google, Pinterest, and Instagram. By typing in your niche or product type into the search bar, you can gauge the overall level of popularity and competition.

- Browse publications like *Woodcraft Magazine, American Woodworker Magazine,* or *Fine Woodworking Magazine* to assess current and upcoming trends in the industry.

- Look at catalogs and other online stores that sell wood crafts, such as Sundance Catalog, Manmade Woods, or Appalachian Spring.

- Browse shops or galleries in your area to see what's selling or on display.

- If you already have followers, run a poll on social media to see what your audience would be most interested in buying.

There are countless sources of inspiration for profitable wood crafts and products. Just be sure to use these as inspiration only—never copy anyone else's work. Instead, pick a product that is already selling and create your own unique version of it.

Product Ideas

If you're struggling to choose a niche or make a list of profitable products, here is a list of wood crafts that generally sell well:

- *Kitchenware* – cutting boards, bowls, utensil sets with holders, engraved spoons, stove top covers
- *Home organization* – pen sets or holders, desk or jewelry organizers, keepsake boxes, key holders, shoe storage
- *Artistic* – abstract sculptures, unique wall art, layered or intricate pieces
- *Furniture* – chairs, stump stools, coffee or end tables, cabinets
- *Outdoor/nature* – birdhouses, animal sculptures, personalized signs, benches
- *Small pieces* – jewelry, ornaments, keychains, carved miniatures

You can choose products from one of the categories above and then use market research to refine your niche. Remember the more specific your niche is, the easier it will be to sell to your ideal customer.

Chapter 3

Branding

Now that you've brainstormed your product line, it's time to think about branding, or in other words, how to make your woodworking business stand out.

As we've mentioned previously, one of the biggest hurdles in the woodworking industry is high competition. In order to achieve a six-figure business, you'll need a distinct brand that will separate you from your competitors.

Your business needs a hook that will reel the right customers in from the start. The goal here is to choose a cohesive brand that appeals to your ideal customer base and then ensure all the elements of your business correspond with that brand.

Throughout this chapter, keep your niche and ideal customer in mind. When choosing the elements of your brand, always ask yourself: Will this appeal to my ideal customers and communicate clearly that my products are for them? If the answer is yes, you've created a winning six-figure brand!

Business Name

Your business name is one of the most important elements of your brand. Ideally, it should be aligned with your niche, so your ideal customers can easily find you. While you may choose to use your own name for your woodworking business, doing so is often a missed opportunity to communicate your brand right up front.

For example, imagine that you're a parent at a craft fair looking for eco-friendly toys for your kids. What's going to stand out to you more: John Smith Woodworks or Nature Based Toys? If your product line is natural wooden toys, the second business name will bring your ideal customer right to your booth!

When it comes to branding, you should aim to clearly communicate what it is that you sell and who your products are for. Your business name is a great way to do this!

Once you've chosen a business name, make sure it's available by doing a business search in your state and checking registered trademarks. If you're planning to have a website, check namecheap.com to make sure the domain name (URL) is available.

Story

As an artisan and small business owner, your story is what makes you stand out from larger stores and corporations. Your artisan story makes you unique and should be shared with customers whenever possible.

Your story should be three to five sentences about how you got started, what inspires you, what makes your products unique, and any other relevant information, such as specific materials you use or your creative process.

As always, keep your niche and ideal customer in mind when crafting your story. You want your story to be authentic, while also relatable to your customers. For example, let's say your ideal customer is a parent looking for unique, eco-friendly toys for their kids. Your story could describe how you personally struggled to find eco-friendly toys for your daughter when she was growing up, so you decided to make your own out of sustainable wooden materials. You can go on to explain how the goal of your business is to share these toys with other parents who have similar values.

Your story can go on your website, Etsy and Amazon Handmade profiles, marketing materials, and more. You can also display or share your story with shoppers at craft fairs and other events to help them get to know you.

When it comes to small business and handmade items, genuine connections lead to sales! Being open and honest about yourself and your journey will draw the right customers to you.

Message

Your message is a 30-second pitch about your woodworking business and who it's for. It can also be described as your elevator pitch.

You can craft your message by filling in the blanks in the statement below:

I sell _____for _____, so they can _____.

An example would be "I sell eco-friendly wooden toys for conscious parents, so they can give their kids the world, while also giving back to the environment."

Once again, as a small business owner, you very often make sales through connections. Your message speaks directly to one specific type of customer and is the basis for your brand.

Logo

Every six-figure business has a logo that reflects its brand. In designing your logo, you should choose fonts, colors, and elements that align with your niche and ideal customer.

When it comes to wood crafts, simple and rustic designs in brown, red, or green colors tend to perform well, but it all depends on your niche. Perform market research by looking at relevant Pinterest boards or the logos of Etsy shops and online stores that are similar to yours. Take note of any common colors or design elements. Use them as inspiration to design your own unique logo that stands out from the crowd.

Your logo can be professionally designed (search for logo designers online or check Fiverr for affordable options) or you can create your own using a graphic design tool like Canva or PicMonkey.

Colors and Fonts

It's important to have a consistent color palette and font style for all business and marketing materials. The goal is for customers who are familiar with your woodworking business to identify your brand at a glance.

Choose colors and fonts that align with your niche and use them consistently throughout all elements of your business, including hangtags, brochures, graphics for social media, and more.

Style

Every profitable brand has a unique style that shines through in photos, booth displays, websites, and more. A consistent style is key to a cohesive and recognizable brand.

For example, if your brand is focused on rustic and natural wood crafts, this style should be reflected throughout your business, including in photo backdrops, website copy, and more.

If you run a sustainable business, this should be highlighted on your hangtags and in promotional materials. If you make eco-friendly products, you should also keep consistency by using recyclable and biodegradable packaging materials.

When it comes to branding, it should always be clear what kinds of wood crafts you sell and who your target market is. This is your best form of advertisement and will draw the right customers directly to you.

Chapter 4

Photography

In this chapter, we'll cover one of the most important aspects of your woodworking business: photography. As the saying goes, "A picture is worth a thousand words."

If you want a six-figure woodworking business, filling your listings, brochures, and marketing materials with gorgeous photos of your products is absolutely necessary. You could be the most adept woodworker in the world, but if your photos are blurry or unappealing, you'll struggle to make sales.

Most popular art and craft shows will judge photos of your work as part of the application process. Galleries and interior designers will expect to see professional photos in your portfolio. When selling online, through Etsy or Amazon Handmade, your photos will be your biggest selling point.

The bottom line is that no matter where you're selling your work, high-quality photos are completely essential to making sales.

Photography 101

All photos of your work should be clear, eye-catching, and professional. Remember, better photos equals more sales.

As with any skill, your photography will improve with regular practice. It's always worth the time and effort to capture beautiful photos that do justice to your work.

Here are some expert tips for taking attractive photos of your wood crafts:

- The right lighting is key to taking great product photos. A continuous lighting kit is ideal for consistent and professional-looking photos, but can be a bit pricey. Tungsten lights are the most affordable type of continuous lighting for those on a tight budget. You can also try a basic light box or ring light, if you sell smaller items. Natural light can work well too—just use light curtains to diffuse the light, so your shots aren't overexposed.

- A DSLR (or digital single-lens reflex) camera will increase the resolution of your photos resulting in beautiful, professional shots. A good, sturdy tripod (we love the Manfrotto tripod kit) can also improve the quality of your photos and give you more control over your shots. If price is a barrier, you can often find gently used DSLR cameras on eBay. Canon makes high-quality and affordable options.

- If you'd prefer to use your phone camera, you can still take beautiful photos with the right lighting and backdrop. Play around with the settings and tools on your phone's camera until you find the optimal ones to show off your work. A mini tripod and add-on lenses can improve your photos, as well.

- Use photo editing software like Adobe Photoshop or Lightroom to spruce up your photos. You can find many tutorials online that show simple ways to get started with these programs. You'd be surprised at how much difference a few simple tweaks to the exposure, brightness, sharpness, or white balance can make to your photos. If you're taking photos on your phone, most have basic photo editing tools built right in.

- When editing your photos, keep it simple! Be sure that your edits don't change or hide the product. You want the photo to look natural and be an authentic representation of your work.

- Photograph your products from all relevant angles, including front, back, sides, top, bottom, or inside, particularly when selling online. Remember that online shoppers can't see or handle the product for themselves—your photos must provide all relevant information needed for them to make purchase decisions.

- Be sure that your photos are the right size and ratio for the platform. For example, on Etsy, photos should be at least 2000 pixels on the shortest side with an aspect ratio of 4:3, while art and craft fairs often have size requirements for photos submitted with your application.

- Never use blurry, unclear, or obstructed photos of your work. If your finger is in the way of the product, don't use that photo. It's well worth the time to retake the picture rather than appear unprofessional.

If you're eager to reach the six-figure mark quickly, high-quality photographs are well worth the time, money, and investment. In addition to regular practice using the tips above, we highly recommend that you consider taking a photography class to grow your skills. You can take classes at local photography schools or online (Udemy has some affordable options).

As an alternative, you can hire a professional photographer to take photos of your work, if your budget allows. While this can be a significant investment, it can save you a lot of time, while ensuring that your photos are polished and your products really shine. This can drastically increase your bottom line in the long run.

A cost-effective way to outsource photography is to hire a student or up-and-coming freelancer, who is willing to work for reduced rates (or sometimes even for free) in exchange for a reference and the opportunity to build their portfolio. You can inquire at your local photography school to find students who may be willing to work with you.

Types of Product Images

You should consider several types of product images for your woodworking business:

1. Product-only photos

These images are ideal for your website, e-commerce store, brochures, and catalogs. Remember to show off all sides, angles, and any relevant details that will help customers make purchase decisions. Use a neutral background, so you don't distract from the product itself.

2. Lifestyle photos

Use props, models, and backgrounds to demonstrate how your product is used in real life. Whether or not you'll need these photos, depends on the type of product you sell.

If you sell sculptures or art pieces this may not be necessary, but if you sell kitchenware or toys, it can increase sales to show how your products are used by real people.

It may also be helpful to include step-by-step photos of how the product is used, if relevant.

3. Artistic photos

For your portfolio or brochure, it can be helpful to have a few artistic shots of your work. Examples are photos that play with light and shadow, use different backdrops, or display your piece in a creative way.

Whether or not you'll require these photos largely depends on your niche, customers, and the types of products you sell. For example, artistic photos can be effective for selling sculptures, but aren't necessary for kitchen utensils.

4. Jury photos

If you're planning to apply to craft shows or fairs, many of them will require you to fill out an application that includes photos of your products. High-quality photos will drastically increase your chance of being accepted into juried shows.

In these cases, professional photos are essential. Choose photos that show off your work with excellent lighting and composition. Make sure your photos show any relevant details and don't include any distracting objects or backgrounds.

Only submit your absolute best images to the jury. If you aren't confident in your photography skills, we highly recommend hiring a professional photographer for these photos.

5. Behind-the-scenes photos

It can be helpful to have behind-the-scenes photos (or even videos) of your work, particularly for social media. Many shoppers of handmade items are interested in how the product is made. These don't necessarily need the same professional touch as your product photos, as they're simply meant to show your creative process.

You should also have at least one professional photo of you as the artist, which can used on business cards, brochures, your website, and more.

6. 3D renderings

3D product renderings are an eye-catching way to increase your online sales, particularly if you sell larger items like tables or chairs. They're great for e-commerce sites, so customers can visualize your product in their home. You can hire affordable freelancers on sites from Fiverr or Upwork to create 3D renderings of your most popular products from photos and dimensions that you provide.

Video

While not quite as necessary as photos, video is playing a growing role in the woodworking industry. Especially when considering your marketing strategy, it's important to note that video content is quickly increasing in popularity and generally enjoys higher visibility on social media than photos or text posts (we'll discuss this in more detail in chapter 9).

Similar to photos, choosing the right lighting, using simple backgrounds, and practicing your skills regularly will improve the quality of your videos. Your videos don't have to be fancy (you can use your phone camera), but make sure the audio and video quality are clear. Short videos (60 seconds or less) typically have the best engagement.

Focus on creating well-branded and engaging videos that speak directly to your ideal customer. You can create videos that introduce your business, tell your artist story, show off your creative process, give customers a behind-the-scenes view of your workshop, and more.

Chapter 5

Packaging and Shipping

In this chapter, you'll learn how to safely package and ship your wood crafts to eager customers who are excited to receive their unique handmade items!

If you're selling online, packaging and shipping are essential to your woodworking business. Even if you primarily sell at craft shows, there may be customers who prefer to have their purchases shipped to them, especially if you sell larger pieces.

Note that packaging is part of branding as well, so be sure to keep your ideal customer in mind throughout this next section.

Packaging

Whether you're selling at craft fairs, on Etsy, or to galleries, it's important to package your products effectively, so they arrive at their destination safely. As a bonus, packaging is also an excellent opportunity for branding and marketing.

When selling in person, it's nice for customers to take their wood crafts home in custom bags or boxes. Not only is this a great opportunity for branding, but it also ensures that their purchases will remain safe until they reach home.

Below is a list of packaging materials that may be useful to your business. The exact materials you need will depend on your brand, the types of items you sell, and the venues in which you sell them. If you sell eco-friendly items, be sure to always use sustainable packaging for your products.

When selling in person, you may need:

- Product boxes
- Bags
- Tissue paper
- Tape
- Custom stickers with your logo on them

When selling to be shipped or transported (i.e., selling online or to a gallery), you may need:

- Any of the above (except for the bags)
- Shipping boxes
- Packing tape
- Packing paper
- Bubble wrap
- Biodegradable packing peanuts (for fragile items)
- Foam or cardboard edge protectors (for large items, such as tables)
- Thin plywood (to protect the surface of large items)
- Fragile tape (for large, fragile items)

In terms of shipping or transporting, the exact packaging materials you'll need largely depend on the size and the fragility of the product. The more fragile your item, the more packaging material you'll need to ensure it arrives to the customer safely.

Here's how to package small to midsize items when selling in person:

> **1.** Wrap items in colorful or patterned tissue paper that matches your brand's style and aesthetic. You can also use plain white tissue paper and affix a sticker with your logo on it to the closure.
>
> **2.** Place the wrapped item in a product box (this is optional, but recommended, especially if the item is fragile). The box can either be custom or plain with your logo sticker on it.
>
> **3.** Place the wrapped and/or boxed item into a custom bag or a plain bag with your logo on it.

You can design custom packaging using services, such as packola.com or noissue.co. Otherwise, you can use plain boxes and bags then add a sticker with your logo or business name on it (this is generally more cost-effective). Always measure your products to confirm they will fit properly in the box or bag before ordering.

In the end, the goal is to send the customer off with packaging that encourages brand memorability. This is an excellent opportunity for advertising that shouldn't be overlooked. Especially at craft shows and other large events, an eye-catching custom bag can bring new customers right to your booth!

Here's how to package small to midsize items when selling products that need to be shipped or transported:

> **1.** Wrap the item in tissue paper and/or place it in a product box as described above.

2. Wrap the item or product box in a layer of bubble wrap for extra protection during shipping.

3. Choose a shipping box that leaves about 1 to 2 inches of room around your product for packing material. To choose the right shipping box, you'll need to measure your product once it's already in the tissue paper, product box, and/or bubble wrap, so you can pick a box with the right dimensions. It's helpful to have a variety of box sizes available for different products.

4. Add about 1 to 2 inches of packing material to the bottom. You can use packing paper or tissue paper for regular products and biodegradable packing peanuts for fragile products.

5. Place your product into the box and add 1 to 2 inches of packing material to both sides and on top. This process ensures that your product fits snugly, reducing the chance of breakage. Always check to make sure that your product isn't touching the sides of the box. If you're shipping multiple items, add a bit of packing material in between to prevent any damage caused by the items knocking against each other.

6. Make sure that your box is taped down securely with packing tape on all sides. You can use two layers of packing tape, if needed.

When shipping or transporting larger items, such as tables or other furniture, you'll generally need to use several layers of heavy-duty bubble wrap. Make sure all corners are covered with either cardboard or foam edge protectors and that flat surfaces are lined with a thin layer of protective plywood. It can also be helpful to wrap the outside of the box with fragile tape to ensure it's handled with care.

In the following sections, we'll discuss how to ship small or midsize items and then, later on, larger items. The shipping process can drastically differ based on the size of item. Feel free to skip to the section that is most relevant to your products.

Shipping Smaller Items

Now that your wood crafts are safely packaged in their boxes, it's time to ship them!

Here's what you'll need to ship your small or midsize wood crafts:

- Scale (a digital shipping scale is ideal, but a bathroom or kitchen scale works too)
- Tape measure
- Printer, paper, and ink (to print shipping labels – if you don't already have a printer, you can often find used ones on eBay for around $50)
- Clear packing tape

In the US, your primary shipping options are USPS, UPS, and FedEx. If you live outside the US, there are many available options for shipping, including Canada Post, Royal Mail, Australia Post, Global Postal Shipping, and more, depending on where you're based.

Regardless of which shipping service you choose, the cost to ship your products will generally be determined by the size of your shipping box and the total weight of your packaged item, as well as the shipping point, origin, and speed.

Before you ship your package, you'll need to weigh it and print a shipping label. Many e-commerce sites, such as Etsy or Amazon Handmade, allow you to print a discounted shipping label directly through their platform. If you're based in the US and selling directly through your own website, Pirate Ship is a licensed e-commerce platform that offers discounts on USPS shipping.

A great option for shipping most small to midsize wood crafts is USPS Priority Mail. The weight limit for this service is 70 pounds, while the maximum size is 108 inches in combined length and girth.

USPS Priority Mail is fast, insured, and you can save money by using free Priority Mail shipping boxes. You can pick these up at the post office or order them online at usps.com. Just be sure that you use these boxes only when shipping with USPS Priority Mail.

If you're looking for a cost-effective option, USPS Ground Advantage generally has longer delivery times, but offers a more affordable rate. In particular, if you're selling very small wood crafts (e.g., ornaments or jewelry), USPS Ground Advantage offers a tiered pricing structure in 4-ounce increments.

Once you've chosen your shipping service, you'll input both the size and weight of your package to produce your shipping label. After it's printed, you can affix it to the top of your package with clear packing tape and you're ready to go!

Shipping Larger Items

If you sell larger wooden items, such as cabinets, bookcases, or dining room tables, you'll need to utilize a freight service for shipping most items heavier than 150 pounds.

Freight shipping is used to transport bulk shipments that surpass the weight and size restrictions for parcel packages. These shipments can be transported by air, ocean, ground, rail, or a combination of these methods.

When using freight shipping, make sure your item is very securely packed in a box with bubble wrap, foam, and plenty of tape on the outside. To prevent damage during shipping, use polypropylene strapping to keep the box intact.

You'll typically want to pack your item on standard wood pallets, which are portable platforms that provide a sturdy base for stacking items. This will ensure the package isn't damaged when it's lifted with a forklift or pallet jack.

In the US, freight shipping services are offered through FedEx, Old Dominion, TFI International, and more. Options outside the US include Eurosender and DHL (Europe), CSA Transportation (Canada), and Transdirect (Australia).

No matter which products you sell or where you sell them, packaging and shipping will likely be an integral part of your woodworking business. The more comfortable you are with the process of packaging and shipping, the more opportunities you'll have to sell your handmade items to a larger customer base and scale your business to the six-figure mark!

Chapter 6
Pricing

When starting a woodworking business, a key question is always, "What do I charge?" This chapter will teach you all the ins and outs of strategically pricing your wood crafts to maximize both sales and profit margins.

When selling your wood crafts, your pricing will typically fall into one of two categories: direct or wholesale. Direct, also referred to as retail, involves selling your products directly to customers via your online store, craft show booth, or workshop. Wholesale, on the other hand, is selling your products to an intermediary or "middleman," such as a gallery or local shop, who will then resell your products to their customers.

A general metric is to charge 2.5 to 3 times your costs for direct sale and 2 times your costs for wholesale, but this can vary greatly depending on market demand, branding, your reputation as an artist, and the types of products that you sell.

The best way to price your wood crafts is to first calculate your costs then perform market research to assess competitive pricing. In this chapter, we'll show you how to do just that!

Costs

When it comes to pricing your wood crafts, the most important factor is your costs. You'll start by calculating the cost of creating, packaging, and shipping (if applicable) the item.

You'll want to factor in the materials used to create your product, such as wood, glue, and accessories. If you're packaging and/or shipping the item, you'll also want to account for additional materials, such as tissue paper, boxes, and tape. When calculating these costs, you should also factor in the costs of the materials being shipped to you or the travel costs associated with picking them up from the store or lumberyard.

We recommend that you calculate your costs per finished item, so if you buy materials in bulk, divide the total cost by the estimated number of items you can make and ship with those materials.

There may be some material costs that are difficult to calculate and must be approximated. In these cases, always estimate on the high end, so you don't accidentally cut into your own profit.

Estimating the cost of lumber can be tricky, as you'll generally have scraps left after completing the project. In this case, you should calculate the total cost of the wood, including any unused scraps.

Next, you'll want to pay yourself (and any hired workers) for the time and labor put into creating the item. This includes the time spent gathering materials, preparing the project, and producing the item.

In general, you want to start by paying yourself $20 per hour and increase that rate as your business takes off and sales rise. If your business grows to a point where you can (and want to) hire production assistance to increase your output, you'll need to factor this in as well.

Next, you'll want to factor in ongoing expenses for your business that aren't directly related to the creation, packaging, or shipping of your item. This could be the monthly cost of insurance, utilities, graphic design services, email marketing, and more. If any of these costs are yearly, you can divide them by twelve to get the monthly cost.

Divide the monthly cost of these expenses by the average number of items you plan to produce in a month. The resulting number will be the average cost of these expenses per item. Add this to the per-item cost you calculated in the previous step.

Finally, add any costs associated with selling your item, such as e-commerce platform fees, credit card processing fees, or payment gateway fees. For example, if you're selling your item on Etsy, there will be a $0.20 listing fee for every four months that your listing is active. Once you make the sale, you will be charged 6.5% of the listed price plus the amount paid for shipping (if applicable) plus a payment processing fee of 3% + $0.25, if you're selling from the US.

Market Research

Now that you've calculated your costs, it's time to perform market research to determine the ideal pricing for your item.

Direct

When selling direct, you should do research on selling platforms, such as Etsy or Amazon Handmade, to see what prices your competitors are charging for items like yours. You can also explore wood craft catalogs, visit local handmade shops, or browse craft fairs to get an idea of pricing in your niche.

Pay close attention to factors such as size, material, production process, and how intricate the piece is. The pricing for a two-inch bird figurine will be significantly different from that of a twenty-inch one. If your piece is particularly intricate or uses an unusual production technique, you should factor that in as well.

As an example, if you're looking to sell a two-inch painted wooden bird figurine on Etsy, a quick search on the platform will reveal that the best-selling items like this are priced between $10 and $18. If you've calculated your cost per item at $5 and you're aiming for a profit margin that is 3 times your cost, you could price your item at $15.

Remember that the standard pricing metric for direct sales of handmade items is 2.5 to 3 times your cost, but it largely depends on your niche and item. In the woodworking industry, every item is unique and you'll have to determine what makes your item similar or different from your competitors then choose your price accordingly.

For example, if you use sustainable materials and your competitors don't, you may be justified in charging a few dollars more than they do. Just be sure that you highlight sustainability in your listing title, so customers understand that your item offers a higher value.

You'll often need to adjust your pricing over time to see what results in maximum sales. Set your price for at least 30 to 60 days and then make small pricing adjustments (5%–10% of your current price) until product sales are consistent.

While decreasing your price can result in more sales, you'll want to be careful with lowering it too drastically. In the woodworking industry, pricing that is too low sometimes decreases the perceived value of the product, which can actually result in fewer sales.

Remember that handmade items are not generic products like toothpaste, where customers are just looking to get the best possible deal. Your wood crafts are a labor of love and your pricing should reflect that. If you're struggling to make sales and find that your prices are significantly lower than your competitors, a price bump might be just what you need!

Wholesale

Stores will typically mark up your products by 2 to 2.5 times when setting their retail price. Galleries usually take commission on your work and the percentage can vary greatly, although 30%–60% is common.

In terms of wholesale, the standard metric is to price your item at 2 times your cost, but the final price will largely depend on what the store or gallery plans to sell your piece for. If they aren't able to hit their desired profit margin, they aren't likely to buy your items.

When selling wholesale, you should research what items like yours are selling for at local stores and galleries to determine your pricing. You can also look at sites that purchase wholesale from makers, such as faire.com or artfulhome.com.

Determine a price that will ensure that you make a profit, while also allowing the store or gallery to mark up your item to their standard price. Be prepared to negotiate, but never accept a price that feels unfair or is too low for you to make a profit.

Whether you're selling direct or wholesale, you should plan to reevaluate your pricing periodically to account for inflation, fluctuating market demand, and your growing reputation as an artist.

Profit Margin

To maximize the income from your business, you'll need to choose a price that's competitive for your niche and also provides you with a healthy profit margin.

If a competitive price for your item results in little to no profit, you'll need to lower your costs. You can often save money on craft materials by shopping in bulk, searching for discount codes, taking advantage of sales, or buying from a different retailer. Popular craft stores like Michaels or Joann regularly offer discount codes through their apps.

In terms of wood, lumberyards typically offer affordable options compared to big box stores like Lowes or Home Depot. Very often the wood will be higher quality at lumberyards and you may even receive loyalty discounts, if you buy in bulk or develop a good relationship with the owner.

If you're able to buy your wood in volume, many sawmills sell cheap lumber to woodworkers at wholesale prices. Just be aware that the lumber will be rough cut, so it's untreated and will carry extra moisture.

Always be willing to adjust both your costs and pricing until you find the sweet spot that results in the maximum number of sales for the optimal profit per item.

Custom Pieces

If you're selling custom, commission, or one-of-a-kind pieces, you can usually charge higher than your standard amount. You can price based on square foot or by the hour, plus the cost of materials, packaging, overhead, and shipping.

Prices for custom pieces typically increase with your reputation and popularity as an artist. When starting out, you can plan to charge 4 to 4.5 times your cost and increase your rates over time, as demand for your custom pieces rises.

Chapter 7

Selling In Person at Craft Shows, Events, and More

A distinct advantage of a woodworking business is the ability to capitalize on multiple income streams. By selling your wood crafts at different venues, both in person and online, you can build a sustainable six-figure business with a dependable income.

In this chapter, we'll explore in-person selling at craft shows, festivals, and other events. This is often a great place for newbies to start because you can make quick sales, see how customers react to your product line, and they're usually a short-term commitment (a few days or a weekend).

In the next chapter, we'll explore selling online, which will add diversity to your business and help you hit that six-figure mark quickly!

Art and Craft Shows

There is a large variety of art and craft shows available for you to sell your products. Some are juried and require an application with images of your work, while others are not. They can also sometimes be called art and craft fairs, festivals, or markets.

Application

Most art and craft shows require an application, particularly popular ones. The most competitive shows typically have nonrefundable jury application fees and vendor applications can be due as early as six to twelve months before the show date.

When applying, read the instructions very carefully taking note of application deadlines, photo guidelines, and rules. There will typically be a specific number of photos that you must submit following their parameters. Oftentimes, this will be three to five individual pieces of your work, as well as a photo or two of your booth display.

Many craft shows throughout the US provide applications through ZAPP at zapplication.org. You can find an application either through the craft show's website, if there's a specific one you'd like to apply to, or you can find shows through ZAPP using their events list or calendar.

While those who are new to the business are sometimes reluctant to apply for juried shows, these are typically the most well-attended and, therefore, the most profitable shows for vendors. If you've taken the time to perfect your work (chapter 1) and improve your photography (chapter 4), you can be in a good position to be accepted into a juried show, even if it's your first!

We encourage you to apply to any show that feels like a good fit for you. If you aren't accepted, don't take it personally! Some of these shows are highly competitive and only accept a modest number of applicants. Simply work on improving your craft and photos, as well as gaining experience through non-juried shows, and then reapply the next year. You can also consider hiring a professional photographer to take your jury images, which can increase your chances of acceptance.

In terms of non-juried shows, they typically fill space on a first-come, first-served basis. Be sure to apply early to secure your spot.

Setup

Once you've been accepted into a craft show, you will be assigned an exhibition space. This space is most commonly 10 feet by 10 feet or 12 feet by 12 feet, but can vary based on the show (you can find this information on the show's website or application).

You will generally be expected to bring your own display booth, racks, lights, and anything else you'll need to properly display your works. Depending on which wood crafts you sell, you may design your booth using portable tables, display pedestals, shelves, or easels.

If the craft show is outdoors, you'll also need a weighted canopy tent. You should look for a tent with straight legs (not slanted) and four removable sidewalls. We recommend KD Canopy, Caravan Canopy, or E-Z Up for reliable canopy tents. If cost is an issue, you can often find one for cheap on eBay, Craigslist, or Amazon (read reviews before buying).

In terms of lighting, you can use overhead booth lighting, puck lights, clip-on lights, or anything else that makes sense for your display. Make sure you have extension cords and are aware of any lighting requirements for each show.

Finally, be sure to have a large and eye-catching sign with your business name on it. Your sign should make clear your niche and what it is that you sell. If the items you sell aren't obvious from your business name, add a few words underneath that highlight your main products (e.g., Becca's Woodcrafts: Ornaments, Crosses, and Nativity Sets). You can also display your artisan's story, message, or anything else in your booth that could draw customers in.

Most juried shows require that you send photos of your booth display as part of the application. Set your booth display up at home first to ensure it looks attractive and professional. You can look at blogs or Pinterest for inspiration. Make sure your booth photos are well lit and showcase your display clearly.

With regard to location, corner booths are highly coveted as you can entice customers in from both directions. A location near the show's entrance or more frequented areas can also be advantageous. While many craft shows don't give you a say in your booth location, some allow you to make requests, sometimes for an additional fee.

Expenses

Nearly all art and craft shows come with vendor expenses. The extent of these expenses can vary largely depending on the popularity and attendance of the show (i.e., more popular shows typically come with higher fees). A small, local show can have modest fees of $10 to $50 per day, while larger shows can have fees of several hundred dollars per day.

Show expenses typically include an application fee and booth space rental fee. You'll also need to factor in parking, gas, meals, or even hotels, if traveling from a distance. You might also need to consider the costs of your booth display and pop-up tent, but these are generally paid for up front and can be used over and over for any show you attend.

Popular shows typically come with higher expenses, but you can expect more sales. Conversely, smaller shows typically have low fees, but sales are not guaranteed.

When deciding whether or not to travel for a particular show, you should carefully weigh travel costs (in addition to other show expenses) against the amount of profit you expect to make based on crowd size, interest, and competition. It's sometimes possible to make more profit at a smaller, local show than at a larger show that requires significant travel expenses.

We recommend experimenting with both local shows and popular shows to see what works best for your business and products. It can be helpful to do as many local shows as possible to start, since expenses are typically lower and you can test interest in your products. In terms of larger shows, you can aim for one to two in your first year and increase the volume as your profits and experience grow.

Recommendations

Here are some of the most popular craft shows, fairs, and festivals in the United States:

- La Quinta Art Celebration in La Quinta, California
- Plaza Art Fair in Kansas City, Missouri
- Gasparilla Festival of the Arts in Tampa, Florida
- Wickford Art Festival in North Kingstown, Rhode Island
- Bayou City Art Festival in Houston, Texas
- CenterFest Arts Festival in Durham, North Carolina

If you live outside the US or would like to sell abroad, here are some great options to consider:

- One of a Kind in Toronto, Canada
- Masterpiece London Art Fair in London, England
- Finders Keepers in Sydney, Melbourne, and Brisbane, Australia
- Indian Art Fair in New Delhi, India
- Liberdade Street Fair in São Paulo, Brazil

There are many well-attended craft shows that aren't on this list, so be sure to do your research. Crafts shows in your area will save you money on travel expenses resulting in a higher profit on sales. You should also consider your niche and ideal customer, when choosing a craft show. For example, some craft shows may be better for selling sculptures, while others specialize in jewelry.

You can find craft shows and other selling events on zapplication.org, festivalnet.com, and artfaircalendar.com. If you're specifically looking for shows near you, check out local publications, your city or town's website, or Eventbrite.

Pro Tips

- If you're intimidated by the prospect of in-person selling and engaging with customers, local selling events, such as flea markets or craft fairs sponsored by churches or schools, can be a great place to start! You won't make a fortune, but it's good practice and a start to getting your brand out there.

- Keep notes about each show that you attend detailing crowd size, sales, costs, and anything else that feels relevant. Only return to the shows that made you the most profit for the amount of time, money, and effort it took to participate in the show. Over time, this will help you build a solid and dependable income.

- Many people don't carry cash anymore, so if you don't accept credit card payments, you'll be missing out on valuable sales. A mobile credit card reader plugs right into your smartphone and pairs with a point-of-sale app. We recommend Square, as it comes with a free reader for new businesses. Other options include Clover Go and PayPal. Be aware that mobile credit services come with per-transaction fees that should be accounted for in your expenses.

- Make sure to always have business cards, brochures, and other marketing materials at your booth. Sometimes people may not buy at the time, but will place an order through your website or Etsy shop later on. You should also encourage all shoppers (whether they make a purchase or not) to sign up for your email list. We'll discuss email marketing in greater detail later on.

- The first rule of in-person selling is to make it easy for customers to make a purchase. This includes adding price tags to your items (or have a price list on display), offering written or printed receipts, and taking credit card payments. You should also be sure to have multiples of your best-selling items in stock, so you don't lose out on potential sales.

- While you can sell larger and more expensive pieces at craft shows, shoppers at these events tend to lean more toward smaller impulse buys. Be sure to have inexpensive items available to sell alongside your pricier ones to maximize your sales and appeal to a diverse group of shoppers. In terms of high-end pieces, your best bet will typically be to sell them through galleries, auctions, or art agents, which we'll discuss further in chapter 12.

- Be personable and share your story with customers. Remember that shoppers often buy from handmade artists because they connect with their message. As people are browsing, say hello, explain your process or materials, and highlight what makes your wood crafts unique. Many shoppers at shows are excited to meet the artist behind the craft and are more likely to make a purchase if you genuinely connect with them.

- Be aware of show hours, setup, loading and unloading procedures, parking arrangements, and any other logistics ahead of time. This will make the process much smoother on the day of the show and ensure you don't lose any valuable selling time. If the show allows set up a day before, definitely take advantage of this too.

Other Selling Opportunities

When it comes to in-person selling, you can maximize your income by thinking outside the box! While art and craft shows have clear demand for wood crafts, there's also often high competition. Since most booths are selling handcrafted items, it can be hard to stand out.

While we still recommend selling at craft shows and festivals, as they can be profitable and provide great exposure for you as an artisan, you're leaving significant money on the table by limiting yourself to just those events. The ability to cast a wider net in terms of selling is often the difference between a woodworker who makes six figures and one who doesn't.

Niche Selling

Selling to your niche means bringing your products directly to your ideal customers. In doing so, you can often overcome competition and draw the perfect customers right to you.

Start by thinking about your ideal customer and which events would draw them in. Refer to your answers from chapter 2 to really home in on who your ideal customer is, where they like to hang out, and where they tend to shop. Research niche-specific events that would be most appealing to your customer base.

Here are some examples:

- Wedding expos

Many weddings have a rustic theme that emphasize earthy colors and organic materials. Weddings with this theme often require custom wooden signs, wood slices as centerpieces, and even personalized wooden hangers for bridesmaids!

If you're planning to sell any of these items, then wedding expos could be a profitable venue for you. It's also a great opportunity to sell custom woodwork, as many brides or grooms may want a unique piece for their special day.

- Renaissance fairs

If you sell items like wooden toys, dragon figurines, or anything else that would fit in a medieval theme, a Renaissance fair is the perfect opportunity to sell your wood crafts. These are typically outdoor events that are well attended and can run for several months, resulting in dependable income.

- Christmas markets

If you sell wooden crosses, ornaments, nutcrackers, or anything else that would make a great holiday gift, a Christmas market can offer a large source of seasonal income to boost your business. Plus, you can connect with customers that may be interested in purchasing more of your products throughout the year.

- Farmers markets

If you sell small wood crafts, particularly food-related ones like wooden salt boxes, utensils, or bowls, well-attended farmers markets can provide a steady customer base. Note that farmers markets are best for inexpensive wood crafts that can qualify as impulse buys. Customers at farmers markets typically aren't generally looking to buy large furniture or expensive art pieces, which is why understanding your niche and ideal customer is so important.

By meeting your ideal customers where they're already likely to make purchases, you're capitalizing on your niche and fortifying your sales.

Business-to-Business (B2B) Selling

By selling your products to relevant businesses, you can generate bulk orders, form long-term business partnerships, and achieve consistent income. Start by thinking about your niche and which businesses could benefit the most from your products. Then, research expos, trade shows, and events that would allow you to network with those businesses.

Here are some examples:

- Restaurant trade shows

If you create wooden kitchen or dining ware, then a restaurant trade show could be a great place to showcase your products. You could sell menu clipboards, check holders, wooden signs, cutting boards, and more. Restaurants often place bulk orders, which could result in earning a large sum of money from just one trade show.

- Interior design expos or trade shows

If you sell furniture, art pieces, or home decor, your business could largely benefit from relationships with interior designers. A great place to start is by attending an interior design expo or trade show, where you can market your skills and make connections.

- Other B2B opportunities

It can often be mutually beneficial to partner with local businesses in your area that may be in need of your products. For example, if you sell custom wooden coasters, you may be able to partner with local breweries to create ones with their logo on them.

To start, make a list of five to ten local businesses in your area that could be in the market for your products and pay them a visit. Share what you love about their business (a little flattery never hurts!) and explain why you think a partnership would be mutually beneficial. Show them the range of relevant products you offer and consider providing them with a sample (e.g., a set of four custom coasters with their logo on it). Be sure to thank them for their time and follow up a week later.

When it comes to B2B selling, it's important to play the long game. A profitable partnership with a local brewery could start with a few dozen coasters and result in a 10-foot custom woodcarving for their entryway! Long-term partnerships can also stabilize your income, so you're not as affected by fluctuating one-off sales.

By thinking outside the box, you can capitalize on opportunities that other sellers in your niche may not have considered. While craft shows will likely have other woodworkers present, you could be the only one selling wood crafts at a restaurant trade show, which effectively allows you to leverage demand with little to no competition. Local businesses are often in search of new suppliers and can be a great source of wholesale income for woodworkers.

In general, you should always be on the lookout for selling opportunities with high demand and relatively low competition. The income potential for these can be staggering and you may discover an amazing source of consistent business that you may not have considered before.

Chapter 8

Selling Online through Etsy, Amazon, and More

While selling in person is a great way to make quick sales, promote your brand, and connect with customers, if you want to make six figures in the woodworking business quickly, you'll generally also need to sell your wood crafts online.

Online selling allows you to reach a much wider customer base and make a large volume of sales, even when you're not actively working. Many six-figure craft businesses are built solely online through popular e-commerce sites like Etsy or Amazon Handmade.

While we encourage you to sell both in person and online to fortify your business and diversify your income, if you prefer to work from the comfort of your own home, you can certainly make six figures by simply leveraging online sales.

In this chapter, we'll discuss the best places to sell your wood crafts online, teach you how to get started, and share key strategies for making an income on each platform.

Etsy

Our number one platform for selling handmade items online is Etsy. It's one of the easiest ways to start selling and get your woodworking business off the ground quickly.

Etsy is a global online marketplace that focuses on handmade, vintage, and craft items. This means a built-in customer base that's already primed to buy your wood crafts.

If you only sell your wood crafts on a single platform, Etsy should be the one. Many sellers make full-time six- or even seven-figure incomes just by selling on Etsy.

In a growing marketplace of over 95 million buyers, your ideal customers are already shopping on Etsy and excited to buy from you! On the flip side, Etsy is a highly competitive platform with lots of experienced sellers and a bit of a learning curve.

In this section, we'll teach you everything you need to get started on Etsy alongside powerful strategies for standing out above the competition!

Getting Started

To open your shop, go to Etsy.com/sell. Once you choose your shop name, put up your first listing, and share payment details, you're ready to start selling. It really is that easy!

In order to stand out on Etsy, you'll want to make sure you have a clearly defined niche and ideal customer. All the products in your shop should have (1) a proven demand on Etsy and (2) been created with the same ideal customer in mind. As the saying goes, "When you speak to everyone, you speak to no one." The same concept applies to selling on Etsy.

As we've mentioned before, Etsy is a huge marketplace with lots of woodcrafters already selling on the platform. If you want to stand out, every aspect of your shop, including shop name, icon (your logo), banner, title, and about section should speak to the specific type of customer you want to reach. Your goal is to create a consistent and marketable brand that attracts the attention of your ideal customer.

Once you open your shop, you'll find that Etsy has many built-in tools to help sellers succeed, such as marketing, analytics, and much more. You'll find all of these user-friendly tools in the Shop Manager (just click on the little icon that looks like a craft fair booth!).

Listings

In order to open up shop, you'll need to put up your first listing. Your listings are simply the items that you have for sale on Etsy.

Your listing needs a strong title containing relevant keywords that your ideal customer is already searching for. You can perform keyword research by searching within Etsy itself and noting which suggestions come up. You can also use an Etsy keyword tool like Marmalead or eRank.

Etsy allows you to upload 10 product photos per listing: one main photo that shows up in search results and nine others. Your photos should be at least 2000 pixels on the shortest side and have an aspect ratio of 4:3 (i.e., horizontal or landscape images). Be sure to follow the guidelines from chapter 4 to ensure your photos stand out. Etsy is a very visual platform and professional-looking photos will increase your click-through rate and improve your sales.

In addition to a title and photos, your listing needs a relevant category and enticing description. You can also add up to 13 tags to your listing that communicate to the Etsy algorithm what your item is and who it's for. Finally, you'll add alt text to make your listing accessible to shoppers with visual impairments.

A well-crafted listing will help the right customers find your products, so you can begin making sales. We recommend starting your shop with five to twenty high-quality product listings and then adding more from there.

Growth Strategies

Below are some key strategies for making sales and growing your Etsy shop:

- *Ask for reviews.* Reviews are very important to your success on Etsy. In general, the more positive reviews you have, the more sales you will make. You can ask for reviews in the order confirmation email and in a follow-up message after the customer has received their item. You can even place a note or card in the physical package thanking the customer for their purchase and asking them to leave a review.

- *Use Etsy's built-in marketing tools.* Etsy has several tools in the Shop Manager that can drastically increase your sales: offering promo codes, running sales, and sending targeted offers to customers who have shown an interest in your products. Don't miss out on these free opportunities to encourage new and repeat business for your shop!

- *Consider paid advertising.* Etsy offers two types of paid advertising through its platform: onsite ads (also known as Etsy ads) and offsite ads. Onsite ads are displayed directly on the Etsy platform itself and can give your listing a more prominent placement on their site. Offsite ads (still run by Etsy) display your products on other platforms, such as Google, Facebook, and Pinterest. Both of these advertising programs can offer a significant boost to your Etsy sales, but need to be factored into your pricing, so you don't lose out on profits.

- *Offer free shipping.* If possible, we highly recommend offering free shipping, especially if you sell smaller items that are inexpensive to ship. Customers love free shipping and tend to perceive it as a better deal. It can even give your listings a boost in Etsy search results! To offer free shipping, simply estimate the cost of shipping the item and factor it into your pricing. Check to make sure that your pricing still aligns with others in your niche once shipping is factored in (if it doesn't, you can attempt to lower your shipping costs by choosing lighter packaging material or experimenting with a different shipping service).

While the strategies in this section are more than enough to get you started making sales on Etsy, we highly recommend our book *Etsy Business Launch* if you want maximize your returns from this platform.

While it's very easy to get started on Etsy, the strategies needed for success could fill an entire book (literally!). In *Etsy Business Launch*, we share our profitable six-step framework that when used in conjunction with this book will ensure you hit the six-figure mark on the platform quickly.

If you're new to selling crafts online, Etsy is a great place to start. It's simple to set up and has a very high income potential. With the right strategies in place, your ideal customers will flock right to your (virtual) door!

Amazon Handmade

Similar to Etsy, Amazon Handmade offers a large base of customers already looking for handcrafted items.

In order to sell on Amazon Handmade, you must first have a Professional selling account with Amazon and then apply to become an artisan through their website (images of your work are required). If you're approved for Handmade, the $39.99 per month selling account fee will be waived, which results in significant savings.

Getting Started

Verify demand for your products on Amazon Handmade by performing the market research detailed in chapter 2. Pay attention to the Best Sellers Rank (BSR) and take note of any bestseller badges in your niche.

Set up your Artisan Profile with your photo, banner, featured products, and story. This will act as your storefront on Handmade and is a great opportunity for branding.

The listing process is similar to Etsy and you can add details about your item's weight, color, size and more. Use specific keywords in your title and description that are well searched on Amazon and relevant to your products. You can upload up to nine images per listing.

. . .

Selling Tips

Many of the tips for success in the previous Etsy section also apply to Amazon Handmade. You should perform market research and create listings that are properly keyworded. Offering free shipping is a common expectation on Amazon and can significantly boost your sales.

Excellent customer service is a must. Respond promptly to all customer inquiries and ensure that shipping times are accurate. You can request reviews five to thirty days after your customer receives their order by tapping "Request a Review" in the order details on Seller Central.

Amazon ads are very effective at increasing your product's visibility on their platform. Sponsored products are pay-per-click (PPC) ads that are easy to set up and typically low cost. Choose 50 to 100 relevant keywords to target for your ads that your ideal customers are already searching for. Start with a modest default bid and make adjustments after two weeks.

Amazon Handmade vs. Etsy

Etsy was started in 2005 and has proven to be a very reliable platform for handmade sellers. Amazon Handmade was established in 2015 and has gained massive popularity and growing numbers ever since.

Overall, Amazon Handmade has higher seller fees than Etsy. Amazon has a 15% referral fee per sale, while Etsy fees are a 6.5% transaction fee plus a 3% + $0.25 payment processing fee (in the US).

Currently, Etsy has 160+ categories to list your item in, while Amazon Handmade only has 14. Etsy also has very detailed analytics showing traffic volume and how visitors arrived at your shop, which can help you determine which of your marketing efforts have the best return.

A potential advantage of Amazon is the option to use Fulfillment by Amazon (FBA). You'll ship your items to an Amazon warehouse, where they will package and ship the orders for you. This results in a more hands-off business model, but can cut into your profits. This fulfillment method is optional and you can choose to ship items yourself.

In the end, the platform you choose largely depends on your products, niche, and customer base. For instance, if you can't find any best-selling items that are similar to yours on Amazon Handmade, it's possible that there isn't enough demand for your niche on the platform.

Etsy and Amazon Handmade have different demographics and what's popular on one platform might not translate to the other. Surveys have shown that Etsy shoppers tend to be on the younger side (25 to 40 years old) and over 80 percent of them identify as female. Amazon shoppers, on the other hand, are more evenly split in terms of age and gender.

While you can certainly sell on both platforms, it can be advantageous to focus on just one platform first and build consistent sales there before branching out to the other platform. Oftentimes, splitting your initial efforts between two platforms can result in mediocre sales from both.

eBay

While demand for handmade items generally isn't as high on eBay as on Etsy or Amazon Handmade, you can still generate a solid income from this marketplace, depending on your niche.

Do your research by entering your products plus the word "handmade" into the eBay search bar and comparing the number of "Sold Items" in the last 30 days to the ones that are still listed. This will give you an idea of what the demand is for your niche compared to the competition. You can also click on the name of eBay sellers that have similar products to yours and sort their listings by "Sold Items" to see how frequently they're making sales.

Since eBay offers 250 free listings per month, it can be worth listing a few items on their site to see how they perform. Once your item is sold, selling fees vary depending on the category of your item and the price that it sells for, but in general, you can expect a 13.75% fee +$0.30 per order when selling from the US.

Like the other platforms, you should upload eye-catching photos that show off your items from all sides and angles, as well as write a detailed and well-keyworded description. Promoted listings (eBay ads) can be a quick way to make sales on the platform and you only pay the advertising fee if the item is sold.

A unique advantage of eBay is that in addition to "Buy It Now," which allows the customer to purchase the item for the listed price, you can also add "Best Offer" to your listing. This allows interested buyers to send you an offer for your item that you can choose to accept, counteroffer, or decline. This can help you move items that aren't selling well faster, as well as allow you to test out a higher price point without risking sales (buyers can still purchase your item for the listed price). Just make sure to set your minimum offer at a price that's high enough for you to still make a profit.

If you're selling a one-of-a-kind piece on eBay, you can also consider auction-style listings, which allow those interested in purchasing your item to place a bid. This can be advantageous if you're unsure of how to price your work, as you may be able to get a high price for it. On the flip side, you don't want your work to sell for too cheap, so be sure to set a reserve price (the minimum amount you're willing to accept for the item). Setting a reserve price will likely decrease the number of bidders in your auction, but will ensure your piece doesn't go for too low of a price.

Your Website

Another option for selling your wood crafts online is through your own website, rather than relying on an already established platform like Etsy, Amazon Handmade, or eBay.

To start your website, you'll first need a domain name and web hosting. A domain name is simply the URL for your business (e.g., naturewoodcrafts.com). You can check the availability of your chosen domain name by going to namecheap.com and entering it into the search bar.

Web hosting is the process of renting space online for your website. There are many inexpensive options for this, such as Bluehost or SiteGround. You'll also need to add a payment gateway, which connects your website to a checkout system, such as Stripe or Square.

If you don't have any experience building or running your own website, it can be a bit intimidating to get started. Luckily, website builders like WordPress, Wix, and Squarespace offer user-friendly interfaces, templates, and customization options. Many hosting platforms offer one-click installation, which helps to simplify the process. Alternatively, you can hire a professional to design your website for you, if you have the funds and want your website to really stand out.

In order to bring customers to your site, you'll need to prioritize search engine optimization (SEO) strategies. This is similar to the keyword research you performed for Etsy, Amazon Handmade, and eBay, but now you're trying to optimize your website, so that it shows up on the first page of search engine results when your ideal customers search for products like yours.

You can perform this keyword research by typing a relevant keyword into Google and seeing which suggestions come up. You can also use free tools like Google Keyword Planner or Google Trends to help you identify the keywords that your ideal customers are searching for. You should choose longtail keywords that are composed of three to five words (e.g., wooden cross for wall).

Use relevant keywords in your title tags, headers, meta descriptions, alt text, URLs, and content to communicate to search engines what your website sells and who your business is for. Just be careful not to "keyword stuff" by adding too many in one place.

An obvious advantage of your own website is that you operate independently and aren't subject to any rules or changes that the other e-commerce platforms make. You can design your website to fit your brand and offer any sales or special promotions that you want. You can even start a blog or have a pop-up form for your email list right on your site. You can also potentially increase your profit margins by avoiding Etsy, Amazon, and eBay fees, although payment gateways still come with their own (generally lower) fees.

On the flip side, it can be significantly harder to gain traction with just a website, particularly when you don't have an email list or customer base for your business yet. While Etsy, Amazon, and eBay come with fees and other caveats, these are in exchange for access to their large, built-in customer bases, as well as marketing tools that help sellers succeed. The users on this platform are already primed to buy and have trust in the platform itself, which can lead to quicker sales and more consistent income.

Overall, we recommend starting with Etsy or a similar platform first, in order to build your woodworking business quickly. Later on, once you have a solid customer base, you can sell through your own website as well. Etsy even has a website option called Pattern by Etsy that syncs with your Etsy shop and allows for further customization.

Social Media

Social media can be a great place to sell your wood crafts, while simultaneously building your brand. Facebook, Instagram, and Pinterest all offer online storefronts where shoppers can browse and purchase your products directly from the platform.

While we don't recommend only selling on social media, it can be an easy extra source of income on top of Etsy, Amazon, eBay, or your own website. Setting up shop on these platforms is simple and generally requires little maintenance.

Start by uploading your catalog of products and setting up your shop on each platform. This is done through the Commerce Manager on Facebook and Instagram, and through Catalogs on Pinterest. You can increase sales and visibility by creating collections and branding your shops.

Other Sites

Here are some other websites where you can sell your wood crafts:

- Handmade Artists' Shop
- CraftIsArt
- indieCart
- Bonanza

If you live outside the US, some options include Folksy (UK), iCraftGifts (Canada), Madeit (Australia), and Authindia (India).

Like social media, these sites can be a great additional source of income and often come with lower fees. Nevertheless, we highly recommend that you focus the majority of your efforts on either Etsy or Amazon Handmade to start, in order to leverage their large customer bases and make sales faster. Etsy, in particular, can be a quick route to significant income for handmade artists and it's very possible to make six figures selling on this platform alone.

Through a combination of in-person and online selling, you can realistically achieve six figures within a few years of starting your woodworking business (possibly sooner, if you're working on this venture full-time). Experiment with different selling platforms and venues to see what works best for your business. Do more of what works and eliminate what doesn't until you've refined your business model for maximum income.

While choosing the ideal selling opportunities for your business is important to your success, it's equally, if not more, important to effectively market your business. In the next chapter, we'll teach you the best marketing strategies that will ensure you make sales, no matter where you choose to sell your wood crafts!

Chapter 9

Six-Figure Marketing

Now that you've chosen your products, perfected your pricing, and decided where to start selling, it's time to market your woodworking business.

With the right marketing strategies, you can easily bring the right customers to your door and even foster repeat business! A profitable customer base filled with shoppers who are excited to buy from you, whether online or in person, is the foundation of any six-figure business. Let's get started!

Marketing Materials

First things first, your woodworking business needs marketing materials.

Some basic marketing materials to have on hand are:

- **Business cards** – These are great to have when selling in person or just in general (you never know when you might need one!). The standard business cards from

VistaPrint are an inexpensive option when first starting out.

- **Hang tags** – Every piece you sell, whether online or in person, should have a hang tag that reads, at minimum, "Handcrafted by your business name". You can also include the primary type of material used, care instructions, logo, or your business URL and phone number on the tag.

- **Coupons** – It's always a great idea to have coupons for your business to encourage repeat sales. You can include these in packages or shopping bags, send them via email, or even send them through postal mail. A standard coupon is 10% off, but you could offer 15% or even 20% discounts for special events like Black Friday. Just be sure that you can still make a profit after the discount.

- **Thank-you notes** – When selling both online and in person, it's a nice personal touch to add a thank-you note to every purchase. This can be enclosed in packages if selling online or placed in the shopping bag when selling in person. In this note, you should thank the customer for supporting your small business. You can also ask for a review or offer a discount on their next purchase.

- **Postcards** – While not strictly necessary, postcards can be an effective marketing tool, if you've been collecting customer mailing addresses. If so, you can send them a postcard a few times a year with new items for sale, coupons, or holiday greetings.

- **Brochures** – Like postcards, not strictly necessary, but good to have, especially if you sell larger, one-of-a-kind, or personalized items that you may not have with you at a craft fair. We recommend full-color brochures with photos and descriptions of your work, as well as a small section about you as the artisan.

You can customize and order the marketing materials above from print companies, such as Moo, VistaPrint, 48HourPrint, or Avery.

In Person Marketing

When selling in person, particularly at art and craft shows, it can be a challenge to stand out from the dozens (or sometimes hundreds) of other handmade artists. Don't worry—we've got you!

Here are some effective marketing strategies that will help you attract more customers and ensure you make plenty of sales:

- **Banners** – Banners and signs can be a helpful way to draw attention to your booth. An eye-catching design on a large banner can help you stand out at a crowded craft show and should be tailored to your niche (colors, fonts, design, etc.) so the right customers can easily find you.

- **Customer engagement** – One of the benefits of selling in person is the ability to speak to and engage with your customers. Don't be afraid to share your story or details about your process and materials with shoppers who come to your booth. Many craft show attendees love the opportunity to engage with the artisan personally. Just be careful not to come off as "salesy" or pushy. Simply be personable and approachable by greeting customers with a smile and answering any questions they may have. Engaging with shoppers also gives you the added advantage of getting to know your ideal customers better, so you can tailor your business and products to them. This leads to even more sales in the long run.

- **Demos** – At craft shows and other events, shoppers love to watch artists at work right in front of them. This can add to your authenticity as an artisan and draw attention to your booth. If you make small items that require whittling or hand carving, you can work on them at your booth for customers to watch. For larger demos, contact the craft show that you're attending to see if space and regulations allow it.

- **Guest book or email list sign-up** – When selling in person, you should always have a guest book for shoppers to leave details, such as their name and postal or email address with their consent to be contacted. Having a list of physical addresses will allow you to send postcards and coupons through the mail, while email addresses will allow you to stay in touch via an email newsletter (more on this later). The ability to stay in touch leads to future marketing opportunities and the potential for repeat business. You can request that shoppers at your booth sign your guest book, but never be pushy about it.

- **Free gifts** – Another way to draw customers to your booth is by prominently advertising a free gift with purchase. This should be small, inexpensive, and easy to make, such as a simple coaster or wooden keychain made from wood scraps that you already have left over from other projects.

- **Shopping bags** – An attractive and well-branded shopping bag can be a great marketing tool, as customers will be carrying your bag with their purchases throughout the rest of their day. If the bags are eye-catching enough, other shoppers at craft fairs and events will keep a lookout for your booth. Be sure that the shopping bag matches your banner, so that interested shoppers can easily find you.

Online Marketing

In this day and age, the internet is essential to successfully marketing any business. Every six-figure woodworking business needs a strong online presence, including social media and email marketing.

Even if you're primarily selling in person, online marketing will bring in new customers and encourage repeat sales. Many customers who visit your booth at craft fairs and other events will have found your business through social media or other online platforms.

Social Media

In this section, we'll present a list of the top social media platforms for promoting your woodworking business and how to make the best use of them. Even if you don't use social media in your personal life, you should absolutely leverage its marketing power for your business.

With social media, there's often an impulse to be everywhere at once, but overall, it's much more effective to concentrate your efforts on the two platforms that will give you the best returns. In choosing which social media platforms to focus on, think about your ideal customer base and where they like to hang out. Each of these platforms draws a slightly different demographic (e.g., Instagram targets a younger demographic than Facebook), so do your research and choose your platforms accordingly.

No matter which platforms you choose, remember that social media is highly visual. Photos tend to enjoy higher visibility and more engagement than text posts, while the popularity of video posts has boomed in the last several years. All of the social media platforms below allow video content, which can be a great way to boost your numbers and sales.

Facebook

Facebook is a very effective way to promote your business. There are two main ways that you can market your woodworking business on the platform: Facebook Business Pages and Facebook Groups.

A business page shares information about your company, such as your phone number, website, and photos, while allowing you to post updates for your followers. It's a great way to announce sales, share new products, or let customers know which craft shows you'll be attending.

A group, on the other hand, is a community that you create around your business and niche. When members post in a group they're typically asking questions, answering questions, or discussing a topic that they're excited about. By starting your own group, your business and products will become that exciting topic of conversation.

We recommend having both of these for your woodworking business, but to focus the majority of your efforts on your Facebook Group since it offers more opportunity for engagement with customers. Groups also generally have better reach (the number of people who see your content) since they're community oriented.

Plan to post in your group two to three times per day with a mix of engagement and sales posts. Engagement posts, such as sharing behind-the-scenes photos of your work, encourage members to like and comment, while sales posts share new products or coupons that encourage members to make a purchase.

You can grow your Facebook Group by mentioning it to customers when selling in person, encouraging existing members to invite their friends, or adding a link to the group on your website. This a great way to stay in contact with customers and encourage repeat business.

Instagram

Instagram is a highly visual platform and a great way to create buzz for your business. You can share photos of your wood crafts, quotes that relate to your niche, behind-the-scenes photos of your woodworking process, and more.

While you won't necessarily make a ton of direct sales through Instagram (users tend to scroll through their feeds and rarely leave the platform), it's very effective at promoting brand awareness and getting people talking about your business. You can also connect with influencers and others who might be willing to help you promote your products!

You should follow accounts that are relevant to your niche, such as local, complementary, or related businesses (e.g., if you sell sustainable kitchen and dining products, you can follow local farm-to-table restaurants). You can also follow other sellers in your niche, as well as their followers. Many of them will follow you back, as they'll likely be interested in your products as well.

Be active on Instagram by posting consistently (once per day), as well as liking and commenting on other users' content. Use three to five relevant hashtags per post to increase visibility.

Pinterest

Although Pinterest is often considered social media, it operates more like a visual search engine. For this reason, Pinterest is typically the best platform for direct sales of your wood crafts.

The user types a query into the search bar and Pinterest gives them relevant Pins (which are essentially visual bookmarks) to either click on or save for later. This process is so effective for selling that a whopping 90 percent of weekly users make purchase decisions on Pinterest.

In order to effectively promote your business on Pinterest, you'll need to:

- *Create a Pinterest Business Account.* This is free and comes with many useful features, such as access to analytics and the ability to run Pinterest Ads.

- *Create eye-catching Pins with both text and graphics.* While photos or videos alone can work well, adding text to your Pin helps you to better target your ideal customers. Also be sure that your Pins are the correct dimensions to maximize visibility in users' feeds. The current optimal size for Pins is 1000 x 1500 pixels, but check Pinterest regularly for any updates. We recommend Canva or PicMonkey for creating Pins.

- *Add relevant keywords to your Pin descriptions.* Perform keyword research on Pinterest by searching for your niche or product (e.g., wooden toys) and seeing what search suggestions come up. Use the most relevant keywords in your Pin description. Just be sure that the description makes sense and you're not stuffing it with too many keywords.

- *Use a Pin scheduler like Tailwind to post your Pins throughout the day.* Once you create your Pins, you'll need to post them to Pinterest. This can be done manually, but it's much easier to use a pin scheduler, so you can post them at regular intervals resulting in more visibility.

- *Consistently share new content and create Fresh Pins.* A Fresh Pin is defined by Pinterest as images or videos that haven't been seen before. Their algorithm increasingly prioritizes Fresh Pins, so keep creating new content to boost views and clicks to your woodworking business.

Email Marketing

Email marketing is the best way to stay in touch with your customers and encourage repeat business. Your email list offers a direct line of communication with your customer base that isn't subject to algorithms or keywords.

While you should always strive to bring in new customers, don't overlook your existing ones in the process. Research shows that by increasing customer retention by just 5 percent, a business's profitability can increase by a whopping 75 percent.

Email marketing allows you to foster loyalty from existing customers, as well as turn casual browsers (such as those who signed your guest book at a craft show but didn't make a purchase) into buyers. It's a powerful form of marketing that shouldn't be overlooked.

To start, you'll need an email marketing platform, such as ConvertKit, MailChimp, or MailerLite. Many of these platforms have free plans with limited features, so you can test them out first.

Growing Your Email List

If you have a website, you can grow your email list by adding a pop-up form that encourages visitors to enter their name and email address. You can also create a landing page (a standalone webpage that allows people to sign up for your email list) and share the link on marketing materials, social media, and Etsy or Amazon Handmade. You can easily create these forms and landing pages by using the templates provided by your email marketing platform.

When selling in person, you can ask shoppers to sign up for your email list via your guestbook or you can even create a QR code that leads to your landing page. You can create a QR code by simply inputting the link into a free tool like QR.io or Adobe Express. Once you have it, just print it out and display it at your booth for interested shoppers to scan!

The most effective way to encourage people to sign up for your email list is by offering a lead magnet. This is an incentive to join your list, such as a coupon or free digital gift. You can set up a trigger through your email marketing platform that will automatically deliver an email with your lead magnet upon sign-up.

Sending Emails

There are several ways to stay in touch with existing and potential customers through email:

1. Sequences

An email sequence is a series of emails that are automatically sent at timed intervals to subscribers on your list. The most common one is a welcome sequence that is sent to a subscriber immediately upon sign-up. If you have a lead magnet, you'll deliver it in the first email of your welcome sequence. You can set up sequences through your email marketing provider with specific rules for when each email is sent out.

Here's an example of a welcome sequence:

Email 1 (sent immediately): Introduce yourself and your woodworking business; deliver your lead magnet.

Email 2 (sent one day later): Share information about your best-selling wood crafts and products (if your lead magnet is a coupon, this email will direct the subscriber toward what to buy, if they haven't made a purchase yet).

Email 3 (sent three days later): Share information about your woodworking process, materials used, artisan story, or anything else that helps customers get to know you; remind them again to use their coupon before it expires.

2. Monthly newsletter

A monthly newsletter is a great way to connect with customers and keep them informed about your business.

Your email newsletter can include a variety of content, such as the following:

- **Business updates.** Share what you're currently working on, ideas for new products (you can even run a poll to see what your customers like best), dates for upcoming crafts shows or events you'll be attending, and more.

- **Artisan story.** Share what inspires you, how you got into the woodworking business, photos of your workshop, or anything else that helps customers get to know you as an artisan.

- **Fun elements.** Share something fun that customers in your niche would be interested in. For example, if you sell wooden cookware, you can share the occasional recipe.

- **Educational tips.** Offer valuable information, such as tips on caring for wooden cutting boards or advice for novice woodworkers.

- **Gratitude.** Thank your subscribers for being a part of your community and supporting your business.

3. Periodic updates

The last option is to simply email your list whenever you have something specific to share like a sale, coupon, or new product. While this is a low-maintenance strategy, it won't necessarily help customers get to know you. It will also likely result in lower open rates since subscribers aren't used to hearing from you regularly.

While a monthly newsletter will go a longer way toward fostering customer loyalty, sending as-needed updates is still a helpful and easy way to promote your business via email.

Overall, the main goal of email marketing is simply to keep your business at the forefront of people's minds, while giving them incentive to keep making purchases from you.

Other Marketing Strategies

Here are some other effective marketing tools for your woodworking business:

- *Word of mouth.* Spread the word and tell everyone about your woodworking business. Start with your immediate circle like family and friends then expand out to people at your workout class, kids' school, or anywhere else that you find the opportunity. Starting your own business is a huge accomplishment, so don't be afraid to be loud and proud. Very often your first few sales will come from your own community!

- *Distribution of marketing materials.* Hand out flyers, coupons, or brochures for your woodworking business at local events or gatherings. You can also post flyers on community bulletin boards and any other spaces designated for promotional materials (just make sure you have permission first).

- *Customer referrals.* You can incentivize both repeat and new business by having a referral program. For example, if an existing customer refers a friend to your business and the friend makes a purchase, they both get 20% off.

- *B2B referrals.* You can also arrange referrals from complementary or adjacent businesses. For example, if you sell wooden kitchenware, you can provide a local restaurant with free utensils and cutting boards, in exchange for promoting those same products to their customers. If an established business that customers already trust advertises using your wood crafts, this can result in a reliable source of sales for you.

- *Affiliate program.* If you have an online store via your own website, an affiliate program is a great way to drive sales. It's similar to a referral program, but casts a wider net. With an affiliate program, content creators (such as bloggers or influencers) place a trackable link to your store that pays them a small commission for each sale they make. You can set the same commission for all your affiliates or create tiers that adjust the rate based on the number of sales each affiliate makes. The commission, which is typically 5%–30% of the sale price, is in exchange for the affiliate's marketing efforts. This allows you to reach a much larger network of customers and can be a more hands-off, or passive, approach to marketing. You can set up your affiliate program through ShareASale, CJ Affiliate, or other affiliate marketing platforms.

- *Collaborations.* Collaboration involves forming partnerships with influencers or bloggers to promote your woodworking business. This is a useful marketing strategy because it not only leads to sales in the short run, but can also boost your social media following and provide credibility for your business, which serves to increase your income over time. Many influencers or bloggers, with smaller followings of 100,000 or less, will often promote your business in exchange for a free product. If you want to collaborate with a larger content creator, you'll typically need to pay them, so be sure to request their media kit up front (this will include their rates and stats). You can find influencers by searching hashtags that are relevant to your brand and then reaching out through direct message. You can also find influencers by using online tools, such as Heepsy or Upfluence.

- *Publicity.* You can often receive free publicity for your business through media outlets, such as newspapers or magazines. You can pitch your story by having a media kit prepared with your artisan story, photos of your work, and a general fact sheet about your business. You should pitch stories with human interest that highlight what makes your business unique. It's not enough just to pitch your business—you need a hook that shows the human being behind the business. An example would be highlighting the eco-friendly nature of your woodworking business and why sustainability is important to you as a business owner. You can find reporters and journalists who might be interested in featuring your story through Connectively or Muck Rack. You can also reach out to local newspapers and niche-related publications (e.g., if you sell wooden cooking utensils, you can reach out to the editor of a restaurant trade magazine with your pitch).

- *Blogging.* If you have your own website for your woodworking business, blogging is a great way to attract new customers. You can provide value-driven posts to those who are interested in your niche by sharing content related to the items you sell. For example, if you sell wooden birdhouses, you could write blog posts about birdwatching since those who are searching for this topic will likely be interested in your products. Blogging is a very effective SEO tool as the proper use of relevant keywords throughout your content can increase the likelihood of your website appearing on the first page of search results. Keeping your website fresh with engaging and relevant content can increase your visibility and bring new customers right to your site. Your blog posts should also include a mention of one or more of your products with a link to purchase them.

- *Giveaways.* Giveaways are an amazing marketing tool for a number of purposes, including creating buzz and excitement around your business. When people sign up for a giveaway, you can ask them to opt into your email list, follow you on social media, join your Facebook Group, and more. Giveaways are super easy to set up through websites like Rafflecopter or ViralSweep. The only caveat is that there are local laws and guidelines pertaining to giveaways, so be sure to do your research beforehand. A notable one is "no purchase necessary," which prohibits you from requiring that users make a purchase in order to enter the giveaway.

With all of these powerful marketing strategies at your disposal, you're well equipped to effectively grow your woodworking business to six figures. This chapter has a variety of approaches and any of them can work, as long as you put in consistent effort. Similar to choosing your selling venues, do more of what works and eliminate what doesn't until your income is steadily growing.

Chapter 10

Business Fundamentals (LLC, Permits, Taxes, and More)

Now that you know where to sell your wood crafts and how to supercharge your sales, it's time to explore the legal side of running your woodworking business.

In this chapter, we'll discuss setting up an LLC, obtaining necessary licenses and permits, choosing insurance, and filing taxes. We'll even discuss funding options, so you can get your woodworking business off the ground quickly without worrying about capital.

If this all sounds a bit overwhelming to you, don't worry! We're here to simplify the process, so you can get your business off to a strong start without the stress or hassle.

Before we get started, we'd like you to know that we are not lawyers, accountants, or financial experts of any kind. This chapter is meant to provide general guidance only and we encourage you to always consult with a professional before making any legal or tax-related decisions for your business.

Most of the guidance in this chapter pertains to US businesses (since that's where we're located), so be sure to do any research that's relevant to your country, if you're located elsewhere. Your federal government's website is generally a great place to start.

Ready? Let's dive in!

LLC

An LLC, or limited liability company, offers many benefits that will protect your woodworking business and help it grow faster.

The primary purpose of an LLC is to maintain a legal separation between your personal and business assets, but there are other benefits as well, including pass-through taxation and an Employer Identification Number (EIN).

Pass-through taxation means business income is only taxed once at the personal level, which ensures that you won't be taxed twice. An EIN will allow you to open a business bank account and apply for a resale certificate, which can give you access to tax-free wholesale prices on your woodworking supplies. You'll also be able to apply for business credit and loans using your EIN, which we'll discuss later in the chapter.

Although there is a yearly fee to maintain your LLC (usually $100 to $300 per year, depending on the state), the tax benefits will likely more than make up for this.

Below is the basic step-by-step process for setting up an LLC. This process can vary a bit by state, so make sure you do your own research and consult a professional whenever necessary.

> **1.** *Choose a name for your LLC.* Make sure the name is available and fits within the naming guidelines for your state. If your LLC

is a different name than your store, you will also need a "doing business as" (DBA) that is your store name (this is a simple process that just requires an additional form).

2. *Choose a resident agent in your state.* Most states require a resident agent (sometimes called a registered agent) when forming an LLC. This is a person or business entity that accepts tax and legal documents on behalf of your business.

3. *File the articles of organization with your state.* This is a simple form that you fill out and mail to the designated department within your state along with any associated fees.

That's it! The process is easier than most people think and is well worth the effort to protect your business.

Please note that the process above is for US businesses, so if you live or operate in a different country, you should research the steps to register your business there.

Licenses and Permits

Licenses and permits are often legal requirements that vary greatly depending on the country, state, or city in which you reside. You should always do your own research or consult with a professional to determine what is necessary in your specific location.

That being said, here are some permits and licenses that are commonly required for woodworking businesses located in the US:

- **Business license** – After registering your business, you can apply for a business license, if your state requires it. This license is typically issued to retailers and wholesalers, so will likely pertain to your woodworking business, particularly if you're selling in person.

- **Zoning permit** – This is a document, typically issued by your local government, that ensures a building is zoned for business use. If you're operating out of your home, a Home Occupation Permit may be required and can be obtained through your local building department. A zoning permit may be especially needed if you're planning to build or use an existing backyard shed for your business operations.

- **Sales tax permit** – Most states require a sales tax permit or license for selling products. This is essentially an agreement to collect and remit sales tax for any products you sell to your state's tax agency. If you're planning to sell at craft shows or events, most of them will require a sales tax permit.

Insurance

When running a business, it's important to protect yourself with the proper insurance. At a minimum, you should plan to have general liability insurance, which covers a broad range of risks including bodily injury, property damage, and more.

It's also highly recommended that woodworking businesses have product liability insurance, as it provides protection in the event that a customer or their property is harmed by your product. If you plan to hire employees, you should look into unemployment or workers' compensation insurance as well.

When choosing insurance, you should check all federal, state, county, and local laws for any requirements. Many insurance companies offer specific policies that cover a wide range of risks, including crafters insurance, home-based business insurance, and small business insurance.

Take the time to shop around, so you can choose the best price and coverage for your business. Make sure you're only paying for what your business needs, so you're not wasting money on anything unnecessary. Some recommended insurance companies for small businesses in the US are Allstate, Farmers, and Hiscox.

Taxes

For many small business owners, taxes can be a confusing maze of numbers and regulations. We're here to simplify the process and help you stay organized, so you can master tax season like a true boss!

First off, we highly recommend opening a business bank account and applying for a business credit card. This will make it much simpler to track your expenses, income, and profits. It will also make it easier to receive funding for your business, which we'll discuss in the next section.

In terms of tax records, we recommend tracking your expenses in a spreadsheet throughout the year, using the process below:

> **1.** Set up a dedicated spreadsheet for your business finances. You can use software like Microsoft Excel or Google Sheets for this purpose.
>
> **2.** Enter every business expense and income source into the spreadsheet. Include dates, descriptions, and amounts for each entry. Categorize them to make tracking easier.
>
> **3.** Update your spreadsheet regularly, ideally as soon as a trans-

action occurs. This will help you avoid the hassle of backtracking when preparing for your taxes.

4. Keep copies of invoices, receipts, and bank statements as supporting documentation. These will be invaluable if you face an audit or need to clarify any expenses.

5. Keep all financial records in a secure and organized manner. Digital storage can be a convenient and space-saving option.

If you stay on top of your expenses and income all year round using this system, we promise that tax season will be infinitely less stressful.

Here are some additional tips to ensure a smooth tax season:

- *Quarterly taxes.* Once your woodworking business generates a significant income, plan to make quarterly estimated tax payments to avoid underpayment penalties.

- *Tax benefits.* Keeping your financial records up-to-date is not just about meeting tax requirements but also about maximizing tax benefits. With accurate records, you can claim eligible deductions and potentially reduce your tax liability. Possible tax benefits for your woodworking business include the self-employment tax deduction, depreciation for your equipment, business use of home (if your business is home-based), as well as potential deductions for your crafting materials, marketing expenses, travel costs (if selling at craft shows), and more.

- *Accountant or tax software.* Consider hiring an accountant for preparing and filing tax returns. It's usually cheaper than you would think and can more than pay for itself. A good accountant can significantly minimize your tax burden by identifying tax benefits and deductions that apply to your specific business. If you're not using an accountant, we recommend tax software like H&R Block or TurboTax. Both of these have services that provide access to expert help for a nominal fee.

While taxes will likely never be your favorite part of running a business (they certainly aren't ours!), the tips and strategies above will make the process much smoother for you and ensure you don't miss a beat in building your six-figure empire!

Funding

When starting any business, the question of funding can be a stressful one. After all, you have to spend money to make money, right?

While a woodworking business is relatively inexpensive to start, especially if you already own a lot of the necessary equipment, you still might require some capital that is beyond your current means.

Unless you have a significant savings account or investment portfolio, it's possible that you may have to apply for business funding. Don't panic! This isn't as intimidating as it sounds. With the right strategies, you can obtain business credit and loans without putting your personal assets at risk.

Here are the basic steps to apply for business credit or loans:

> **1.** *Obtain an EIN.* By structuring your woodworking business as an LLC, you'll be able to apply for business credit using your Employer Identification Number (EIN) instead of your Social

Security Number (SSN). In doing so, you'll prevent any financial issues in your business from affecting your personal credit.

2. *Optimize your fundability.* If you want to receive approval and favorable terms for business credit cards or loans, you'll need to create a creditworthy business presence. This means that your business must appear both professional and congruent on all fronts. You should also access your business credit reports with the three major credit bureaus (Dun & Bradstreet, Experian, and Equifax) and monitor your scores regularly.

3. *Apply for net 30 trade credit.* Before you can receive business credit cards and loans with no personal guarantee, you'll need to establish your business credit score through trade credit. This can be a very useful way to obtain equipment, materials, and more for your woodworking business. Many suppliers offer trade credit to new businesses with net 30 terms, which means that you can make a purchase directly from the vendor and you have 30 days to pay them back. This is an easy way to obtain the supplies you need to start your business and you may even find that you don't need credit cards or loans with this system. You should try to choose vendors who report to the three major credit bureaus, so you can also build your business credit score in the process.

4. *Apply for business credit cards or loans.* If you require more capital beyond what trade credit can offer your business, you can apply for credit cards or loans. There are many business credit cards and lenders that allow you to apply for funding with just your EIN, which helps you build your business without worrying about your personal assets.

If you're looking for more in-depth guidance, in terms of business funding, be sure to check out our book *The Insider's Guide to Business Credit Using an EIN Only*. This short but comprehensive guide will teach you the exact steps for easily obtaining funding for your woodworking business without putting your personal assets at risk.

We hope this chapter showed you that the technical side of running a woodworking business doesn't need to be complicated. Honestly, the hardest part is simply getting started. You'll be glad you did and your business will thrive because of it!

Chapter 11

Scaling to Six Figures

In this chapter, we'll discuss how to take your woodworking business from just starting out to next level. We'll present our best strategies for scaling your business to six figures, so you can pursue your passion and bring home a sustainable income.

Speed It Up!

One of the fastest ways to hit six figures is to increase your output. The more items you sell, the more money you'll make! Once you have enough demand for your wood crafts, it's time to speed up your production process.

To start, determine your current production capacity. How many items can you make per week? Are you producing quickly enough to keep up with demand for your products? If the answer to the second question is no, you're leaving money on the table and need to increase your productivity.

Here are some tips for boosting your production speed:

- *Invest in better tools or equipment.* Investing in the best tools for your craft will help you work more efficiently. Specialized equipment, such as track saws, orbital sanders, and auto-adjust clamps can help with this. Although they cost some money up front, these tools are investments for your business and will make you significantly more money in the long run. As a bonus, there are often tax benefits associated with new tools and equipment, such as deductions and depreciation. Also, don't overlook basic tools, such as pencils and measuring tape, which can make your job easier.

- *Keep your blades sharp.* This safeguards against injury, while ensuring that your cuts are precise and your products look professional. Checking that your blades are sharp before working on your inventory will speed up the process and ensure that things go smoothly.

- *Set up your space for success.* Increasing efficiency can sometimes be as simple as keeping your workshop organized and tidy. Make sure your space is well lit and set up for safety (nothing slows you down like an injury!). Know where all your materials are and ensure you can reach them easily. Make sure your workshop is big enough to accommodate all your projects and make upgrades, as necessary.

- *Plan ahead.* Be sure to plan ahead for the amount of inventory you plan to make in a given time frame. Always know the quantity of wood and other materials needed to create your products (overestimate, if needed). Nothing slows you down like having to run to the lumberyard because you didn't pick up enough wood to create your batch of inventory. Plan to have extra materials around, in case of mistakes.

- *Choose products that you can make and replicate easily.* You should always have a few products in your inventory that are quick and easy to make. For example, you can make custom signs quickly using a CNC machine. Custom signs are popular and can generally be sold at a high profit margin, which will give your overall business a boost. As mentioned in chapter 1, keeping a production logbook will also make it much easier to recreate products later on.

At a certain point, you may need to outsource in order to scale your business. If you're looking for production assistance, you can visit a community woodshop or woodworking class in your area to find affordable help. You can also post the job online and screen candidates directly from the posting site.

You can likewise consider outsourcing other aspects of your business, such as marketing, graphic design, accounting, or photography. When choosing what to outsource, hire out your most difficult or time-consuming task first, as this will improve your efficiency the most.

When you're ready to hire for your business, you can find many viable candidates on Indeed or LinkedIn. For affordable freelance work, we recommend Fiverr or Upwork. Be sure to properly vet potential candidates by assessing their qualifications, conducting interviews, and checking references.

Boost Your Profit Margin

If you want to grow to six figures quickly, you'll need to accomplish two things: (1) increase production (which we discussed in the previous section) and (2) increase your profit margin. In other words, you'll need to sell more items AND have a higher profit margin per item if you want to dramatically increase your bottom line.

There are two ways to increase your profits: lower your costs or raise your prices. We'll discuss each one in turn in the following sections.

Lower Your Costs

When it comes to lowering your costs, every little bit helps! Even decreasing your material costs by a dollar or two per item adds up if you're selling several hundred items per month.

To lower your costs, always be on the lookout for coupons, discounts, and sales. Shop around to find the best suppliers and prices for your materials. Many suppliers offer trade discounts for buying in bulk.

To save even more, you can buy your materials and equipment on a credit card that offers cash back. Even a 1%–3% cashback adds up over time and can boost your profit margins. With the Ink Business Unlimited Visa from Chase or the Business Advantage Unlimited Cash Rewards Mastercard from Bank of America, you can earn 1.5% back on your purchases with no annual fee.

Raise Your Prices

In order to raise your prices, you'll need to increase the perceived value of your products. This is your ideal customer's perception of your product's merit or desirability.

As your business gains popularity and your reputation as an artisan grows, you can plan to increase your prices accordingly. You can increase the perceived value of your products by improving your woodworking skills (especially when it comes to finishing), offering customization, or including eye-catching design elements.

Increases in prices should generally be small (5%–10% of your current price) and measured. If your production process is efficient and you're selling a significant quantity of items per month, even a $1 raise per item can increase your bottom line. Especially when paired with lowering your costs, you can consistently boost your income with incremental changes to your pricing.

As discussed in chapter 6, lower pricing does not necessarily equate to more sales. In fact, too-low pricing can often decrease the perceived value of your work. Don't ever charge less than you know your products are worth. As long as your wood crafts are high-quality and desired by your niche, the right customers will be willing to pay for them.

Expand Your Business

There are many ways to expand your business and scale to six figures. This is where you can get your creative juices flowing by considering more ways that you can serve your ideal customer through your business.

For starters, you can diversify your inventory by regularly offering new products or starting a new product line—just be sure that anything you choose aligns with your niche and current customer base. You can even run polls on social media or through email to see what your customers would be most excited to buy from you.

You can also easily expand your inventory by offering variations of your best-selling products. For example, if your wooden blue jay figurine is already selling well, you can increase your sales by adding a greater variety of bird figurines to your inventory. If there is a particular product that is quick and easy for you to make (such as custom signs) and desired by your niche, you can significantly increase your bottom line by offering these as well.

It also pays to get creative with the types of offerings in your business. Here are some examples:

- *Online or in-person woodworking classes.* This is a great way to earn extra income, while sharing your skills and expertise. You can offer live classes in person or online, which can often draw new customers to your business. You can also consider prerecorded classes that you create just once and can sell many times over resulting in a passive income stream for your woodworking business. We recommend Teachable or Thinkific for hosting your online course.

- *Digital products.* Similar to a prerecorded class, the magic of digital products is that they can provide passive income. You make them once and then sell them over and over again with little to no additional effort on your part. You can sell DIY woodworking plans, a short woodworking guide for beginners, laser cut files, or anything else that would appeal to your niche.

- *Complementary products.* You can increase your bottom line by selling complementary products that those interested in your current products and niche might be looking for. For instance, if you sell wooden kitchen utensils, you could also sell high-quality olive oil either as an affiliate or by purchasing from a local wholesaler to sell directly to your customers.

- *Personalized products.* This is an easy way to increase your profit margin on many products, such as signs or jewelry boxes. You can charge extra to personalize your products with names, dates, or custom messages.

The more you expand your offerings, the more you can scale your income. Just be sure that what you're offering is something your ideal customer is looking to buy. Always perform market research to validate the profitability of your idea before offering anything new.

Sell Wholesale

As discussed previously, wholesale is when you, as the supplier, sell your products in bulk to a retailer, who then sells your products to their customers. Wholesale retailers can include stores, websites, catalogs, and even galleries or interior designers (we'll discuss those in the next chapter).

Selling wholesale is a great way to expand your business because it's a reliable source for bulk orders. Although the profit margin for wholesale will be lower than retail, you'll make it up in volume. A retailer who orders from your business regularly is a valuable source of dependable income that shouldn't be overlooked. Just make sure you're using the pricing strategies from chapter 6 to ensure you're making an acceptable profit with every order.

You can find wholesale buyers for your business by searching on LinkedIn or approaching local stores or galleries that sell products similar to yours. Be sure to have a brochure and price list ready to present whether online or in person.

Here are some other online resources that allow you to connect with wholesale buyers:

- IndieMe (US and Canada)
- Creoate (US and Europe)
- Wayfair (US, Canada, Europe, and others)
- Faire (US, Canada, Europe, and Australia)

If you're interested in selling through catalogs, you can consider Sundance Catalog or The Vermont Country Store.

Follow the Money

One of our best pieces of advice for scaling your woodworking business is to follow the money. While this may sound obvious, it's easy to get caught up in the daily grind and forget to evaluate the profitability of your overall business strategy.

There's a notion in business known as the 80/20 rule, or the Pareto Principle. It basically translates to 80 percent of your profits typically come from 20 percent of your efforts. This means that you can effectively grow your income by focusing on the 20 percent of your business that yields the most overall profit. In order to identify this 20 percent, you'll need to try different approaches and pay attention to your results.

For example, let's say you sell your products through crafts shows and an online store. If you sell at five craft shows in a year and only two of them yield more profit than your online store, you should drop the three less profitable shows and focus that time on growing your online store instead.

Similarly, let's say you're selling wood crafts on Etsy, eBay, and Amazon Handmade. If you find that Etsy is responsible for the majority of your sales then you should be focusing most of your efforts on growing your profits from that marketplace.

With the strategies outlined in this chapter alongside a willingness to innovate and adapt, you could very well hit the six-figure mark within the first few years of running your business. Remember to work smarter, not harder. Stick with it and you'll see results!

Chapter 12

High-End Selling (Galleries, Interior Designers, and More)

In addition to the strategies discussed in the previous chapter, one of the best ways to scale your income is high-end selling. This means selling to galleries, interior designers, and more.

This may not apply to every woodworking business, but if you sell artistic pieces (such as sculptures), custom furniture, or unique home decor then this strategy can help you achieve six figures and beyond. In fact, many woodworkers who sell high-end work can make thousands of dollars from just one piece!

Ready to get started?

Selling to Galleries

An effective way to receive a large payday from a unique or one-of-a-kind piece is to sell it to a gallery. Well-respected galleries can procure high prices for beautiful woodwork.

Always do your research first to make sure your piece is a good fit before approaching any gallery. Once you've made a choice, call or email to schedule an appointment with the gallery owner. Be ready to present your work and yourself, as the artist, in a professional manner.

You should come prepared with your portfolio, your artist story, and a brochure, along with a printed sheet with your terms and pricing. If you have any press clippings or media mentions, you should include those as well. You should also mention anywhere else that your work has been displayed or sold.

Here are some important questions to ask, when meeting with gallery buyers:

- Will you buy my work outright or is the sale on commission? If selling on commission, what is the percentage?
- How long will it take to get paid after the sale?
- How will you promote my work?
- Is there a commitment? If so, how long or how many pieces?
- What happens to unsold work?

In general, you shouldn't have to pay anything up front for a gallery to choose your piece. Be wary of vanity galleries that charge artists to display their work, as galleries like this have no incentive to actually sell your art.

If a gallery agrees to sell your piece, there will typically be a contract involved. Be sure to review the contract carefully and consult with a lawyer, if needed. Be prepared to negotiate on price or commission, but never accept anything that feels drastically low or like you're being taken advantage of.

Your first sale to a gallery is mostly about getting your foot through the door. Once you've sold to a gallery once, you have an increased chance of selling to the same one or others in the future.

To improve your chance of selling to a gallery, aim to have your work featured in one or more publications using the publicity tips in chapter 6. Galleries are often looking to display work from up-and-coming artists who are already making a name for themselves. Be sure that your portfolio showcases only your best work and invest in professional photography to ensure your pieces shine.

As your popularity and reputation grow as an artist, you can increase your chance of a gallery sale, achieve more favorable terms, and secure higher prices for your work. Remember that patience and persistence pay off!

Working with Interior Designers

If you sell custom furniture or home decor, forming a partnership with an interior designer is a great way to increase your bottom line. You can generally make significantly more income selling through an interior designer than at a craft show. This is because clients who can afford interior designers are often willing to pay top dollar for custom or high-end wood pieces.

When partnering with an interior designer, they may purchase your work up front when decorating a client's home or ask you to create a piece that matches the client's aesthetic. Be prepared to create custom work and be flexible about the requirements. Similar to gallery selling, the interior designer will typically take a commission for selling your work.

You can find interior designers near you through a Google search, LinkedIn, or on social media. When reaching out, send a professional message introducing yourself, presenting your work, and asking if they'd be interested in collaborating. It can also be helpful to include a few professional photos of your work, so they can get an idea of your style and artistry.

If you're already working with an architect or real estate agent, they can often refer you to an interior designer, who may be interested in selling your work. You can also find interior designers to collaborate with at trade shows or industry events.

You can explore artfulhome.com to get an idea of what interior designers are looking for and how to price your work. Remember that you are selling a lifestyle when you work with interior designers, so be sure to tailor your marketing message accordingly.

Other High-End Selling

Here are other opportunities for high-end selling with tips for getting started:

- *Real estate.* There are many players in the real estate industry who may be looking for skilled woodworkers, particularly architects, real estate agents, and building contractors. Examples of architectural woodworking include built-in shelves or cabinets, molding, fireplace mantels, and more. If you are able to take on these types of projects, a contact in the real estate industry can provide a steady stream of work. You can connect with real estate professionals through LinkedIn, a local real estate office, or relevant contacts you already have, such as an interior designer.

- *Auctions.* Both local and international auction houses sell one-of-a-kind art pieces, particularly sculptures. Enthusiastic bidders can easily drive prices up and there is potential to make a large sum of money just from one piece. Bonhams, Phillips, Sotheby's, and Heritage Auctions can command extremely high prices for art pieces, but typically only work with artists who are well-known and highly coveted. To start, you can look into Artsy, LiveAuctioneers, or search for art auctions in your area.

- *Art Agents.* If you create fine art or high-end wood pieces, an art agent can promote your business, sell your pieces, and get your portfolio in front of the right buyers. A good art agent with the right connections can really make your income and reputation as an artist soar. Find a reputable art agent by asking buyers, collectors, and other artists for recommendations. Be careful when searching the Internet for art agents—always get a referral or recommendation for anyone you're considering working with. Typical commission rates for art agents are 10%–20% of the piece's sale price, but can vary greatly.

Keeping an eye open for high-end selling opportunities is a great way to scale your income and make more money from your wood crafts than you ever imagined. Be patient as it can take some time to sell to a popular gallery or connect with a reputable interior designer, but once you do, your income potential can soar very quickly. Just be persistent and don't give up!

You Can Do It!

Congrats! You've made it to the end and are ready to confidently build your six-figure woodworking business. We're so excited for you!

Just a few quick words before you go:

- *Start today.* Your six-figure woodworking business will only happen if you take action! Although this book has all the strategies and guidance you need to be successful, simply reading it isn't enough. Don't procrastinate—take one small step today and keep going until you reach success!

- *Keep in touch.* We're so excited for you to start your woodworking business and would love to support you on your journey. Just go to boundlessbooks.ck.page/woodworking to sign up for our email list. We'll send you our occasional (and very helpful) newsletter with business tips, encouragement, and new book releases!

- *Pay it forward.* If you found our book helpful in any way, we'd be absolutely thrilled if you could leave a quick rating or review on Amazon. This means the world to us and helps the right readers find our book. From one small business owner to another, thank you for paying it forward!

- *Don't give up!* Starting a business is a huge endeavor that takes persistence and resilience. No matter what—do not give up! The journey to six figures isn't always easy, but it's worth it. Believe in yourself and follow your passion. You'll get there!

We wish you all the success in the world. Thanks for being here and good luck!

Other Titles by Alyssa and Garrett Garner

Etsy Business Launch: The Complete Guide to Making Six Figures Selling on Etsy (Start a Craft Business)

Candle Making Business: How to Launch a Thriving Six-Figure Candle Business from Home (Start a Craft Business)

The Insider's Guide to Business Credit Using an EIN Only: Get Tradelines, Credit Cards, and Loans for Your Business with No Personal Guarantee

Launch Your Notary Public and Loan Signing Agent Business: Earn Six Figures Working on Your Terms and Schedule

Resources

Connolly, B. (2023). "Amazon Handmade vs Etsy: 2023 Comparison Guide." Retrieved from https://www.junglescout.com/resources/articles/amazon-handmade-vs-etsy/.

FedEx. (2024). "How to Ship Using Pallets." Retrieved from https://www.fedex.com/en-us/shipping/freight/packing-guide/pallets.html.

IBISWorld. (2024). "Wood Product Manufacturing in the US – Market Size, Industry Analysis, Trends and Forecasts (2024–2029)." Retrieved from https://www.ibisworld.com/united-states/market-research-reports/wood-product-manufacturing-industry/.

Shopify Staff. (2022). "Amazon Handmade vs. Etsy: Seller Pros and Cons." Retrieved from https://www.shopify.com/blog/amazon-handmade-vs-etsy.

Smith, R. (2024). "8 Woodworking Tips to Boost Your Efficiency." Retrieved from https://hardwooddistributors.org/postings/8-woodworking-tips-to-boost-your-efficiency.

Tardi, C. (2023). "The 80-20 Rule (aka Pareto Principle): What It Is, How It Works." Retrieved from https://www.investopedia.com/terms/1/80-20-rule.asp.

TRUiC Team. (2024). "How to Start a Woodworking Business." Retrieved from https://howtostartanllc.com/business-ideas/woodworking.

About the Authors

Alyssa and Garrett are married entrepreneurs who have built successful businesses across multiple industries.

Over the years, they've discovered a practical and reproducible framework for building highly profitable businesses in a short amount of time. Now, their passion lies in teaching budding entrepreneurs how to escape the grind and find financial freedom doing what they love.

When they're not building their entrepreneurial empire, Alyssa and Garrett enjoy traveling, ballroom dancing, and Broadway shows.

Thanks for reading!

www.ingramcontent.com/pod-product-compliance
Lightning Source LLC
Chambersburg PA
CBHW071931210526
45479CB00002B/635